MW01169911

Tears that changed a Nation

Charles L. Tucker

Copyright © 2016
by Charles L. Tucker

All Rights Reserved
Printed in the USA

Printed by
Remnant Publications
649 East Chicago Road
Coldwater MI 49036
517-279-1304
www.remnantpublications.com

Cover Design by David Berthiaume
Text Design by Nicole Warren
Additional Design by Greg Solie • AltaGraph

ISBN 978-1-63452-774-3

About the Author

Charles L. Tucker was born and raised in Coldwater, Michigan. He was the third son in a family of four boys and four girls. He was taught to work at an early age, pulling a wagon with fruit and vegetables door to door, up and down the streets of Coldwater, then working in the fields, station, and store.

Tucker's schooling was in Coldwater, after which he married to a local girl, Arlene R. Schulmeyer. After serving in the U.S. Navy during World War II, he decided to go into religious work. He attended Marion College in Marion, Indiana, Spring Arbor College in Spring Arbor, Michigan, the University of Chattanooga, Tennessee, and Emory University in Atlanta, Georgia. The Tuckers have one son, Terry Tucker of Nappanee, Indiana.

While attending college, Charles worked serving the church and the community in Dalton, Georgia by running the Federal Food Program for the poor and homeless, and by working with problem youth and jail inmates and chain gang prisoners. He was given "The Young Man of the Year" award, and two years later, he was nominated by the Atlanta Constitution newspaper for the top ten young man of the nation.

Mr. Tucker has been a very successful businessman over the years, owning and operating companies in Kissimee, Florida and Nappanee, Indiana.

Table of Contents

Acknowledgments

I want to thank, first of all, the people of the Cranston Memorial Presbyterian Church in New Richmond, Ohio for allowing me to use a journal of the history of the church to write the story of Arminta O'Banion, slave girl who lived to be 111 years old.

Also, I admire and appreciate the hours put in by Marcia Butters, retired high school English teacher from the Homer Community Schools in advising, researching, organizing, and typing so that I might fulfill the desire to bring together a book of this kind.

This is a true story, carved out from old books, newspapers, church records, and old files in libraries, as well as museums and articles, for one hundred and fifty years. You will find this book historically refreshing with new data, pictures, and facts. Tears, emotions, and heartaches of those dark days. The records tell us that slavery created a terrible cancer that wounded the heart and soul of America for generations in both the North and the South. This story is based on the known facts of a slave girl who lived to be 111 years of age, Arminta O'Banion, called Minty.

The excerpt of the following article is from the Cranston Memorial Presbyterian Church in New Richmond, Ohio, a church that took an early and uncompromising stand against slavery. (Picture from Cranston Memorial Presbyterian Church's Internet site).

ARMINTA O'BANION, Born January 6, 1788; Oldest Inhabitant of Ohio

"There are few persons in New Richmond who did not know and respect Aunt Minty O'Banion, not only from her great age, but from the excellence of her character; and all regret her death last Friday, January 6, on which day she had reached the marvelous age of 111 years and 6 days, as shown by authentic records. She has lived through every administration from Washington to McKinley, and noted every war from 1812 to 1898 … up to the last few month of her life she was quite active and frequently seen along the river picking up driftwood and baskets of chips …" *(Excerpt from her obituary)*

Where do we begin with our story? First of all, the article brought forth many questions needing answers, so a good place to start was a travel to the South along the great Ohio River and Mason-Dixon Line trying to visualize and realize the pain and suffering that the slaves had to endure while struggling with hope for freedom into the free states and Canada.

INTRODUCTION

At the time Arminta was born, slavery had already become established in America. The first cargo ship of thirteen Africans arrived in St. Mary's City in 1642, and in 1664, Maryland legalized slavery. In 1783 Maryland prohibited the importation of slaves. The Maryland Gazette denounced the inequality in newly formed America, which promoted liberty and freedom while enslaving thousands.

Turn your reading light up, or light a candle as was used in the 1800's. Throw a log into the fireplace, get a large cup of sassafras tea, sit down in your favorite chair, take a deep breath, and let us begin. See the life of our Minty as being unusual, rather than a reflection of the lives of many other slave women. See through her the events and personages which caused the shedding of tears, tears that brought changes to the nation. See her long life as she remembered it while picking up her wood chips along the shoreline of the Ohio River. See history as seen through her eyes.

Chapter One

Meeting *Minty*

It was December 14, 1799 when the first president of the United States, George Washington, died at his home at Mount Vernon, in Virginia. Two days before his death, a healthy Washington had been riding his horse in the wet, cold snow and rain, arriving home exhausted. He was attacked with quinsy, better known as acute laryngitis. He had been bled heavily four times, given gargles of "molasses, vinegar, and butter", and had a blister pack, a preparation of dried beetles, placed on his throat and chest. His strength continued to rapidly weaken, and he died at 9:00 p.m.

The nation was stung. Tears from saddened hearts were felt in every walk of life. The slaves loved this man with all their hearts, bodies, and souls. Let me introduce you to one of them, Arminta.

George Washington, First President of the United States

According to the Clermont County, Ohio newspaper reporting and the Cranston Memorial Presbyterian Church, Arminta was the eleven year old slave girl on one of the plantations of Peyton Randolph, who was one of Washington's closest friends. Minty, as she was called, was heartbroken. Her tears would not stop. How well she remembered witnessing the pomp and ceremony of his funeral.

How could Minty have been so familiar with happenings at the Washington home at Mount Vernon? To answer this question we must travel back into her past and bring her up to this point in her history.

Masonic Sketch of Washington's funeral

Nine year old Minty had been gifted to Susan Randolph who became her young mistress. Susan Randolph was a dear friend of Martha Washington's granddaughter, Nellie Parke Custis. Susan frequently visited Nellie at Mount Vernon, often spending several days. Because of distance and means of travel, it was customary for company to be entertained for up to a week or more. And since a personal slave accompanied her mistress, this allowed Minty to become well acquainted with the Washington family and their domestic slaves. She would never forget seeing the president smiling at her or giving her a pat on the head.

Little did Minty realize that many of the individuals and events one meets only through history books would actually become a part of her life, people

Painting of Mount Vernon by Jennie Bellows Millards

she would actually see at their worst and at their best, hear their endless debates and nonsensical chatter, wait on their needs and whims, and even witness their joys and sorrows. She would live through every administration from Washington to McKinley, note every war from 1812 to 1898, and witness many heartrending situations, such as the Underground Railroad, the Civil War, and the assassination of Abraham Lincoln. As we travel the road of 111 years that Minty traveled and as we watch her on her own journey, take note of the events that brought about change for the slaves, changes that brought added sorrow to these unfortunate human beings, as well as changes that attempted to improve their lives. The stories Minty could tell.

Many are the times she must have prayed a prayer for her fellow slaves similar to this one:

Nellie Parke Custis

TEARS THAT CHANGED A NATION

Oh, Lord, why must we black people
be slaves to masters?
We did not choose our masters
who have the right to beat us
until blood runs down our legs.
We did not choose our color.
We did not pick our fathers and mothers.
We did not choose where we would live,
work, or die!
Oh, Lord, we are chained, shackled,
and hauled to the cities
To be sold on the auction block
like pigs, cattle, sheep, and horses.
We have no name, nor rights.
We are property of the masters.
Oh, Lord, oceans of tears stain our cheeks
when we are beaten,
but most of all, when our families are
split up
and sold to strangers, never to be
seen again.

Charles L. Tucker

Chapter Two

Minty's First Master,
Edmund Randolph

As the elderly, wizened Minty meandered along the shore line of the Ohio River filling up her basket with wood chips, her mind often wandered back over the years recalling the things she had learned along the way, and how she became Aunt Minty.

Thoughts of her first home, the only home she had known during her first twelve years, often invaded her mind, flooding her eyes with tears. Her mother. Her father. Her siblings. Whatever had become of them? Were their names Randolph as hers must have been? Her family name must have been Randolph because she had been a slave on a plantation of Peyton Randolph in Virginia. She had been born, on January 6, 1788, just nine short miles from Mount Vernon.

As her childhood progressed, she learned much about her first master from her mother and the other slaves. Peyton Randolph, Washington's best friend, is considered our first president of the Continental Congress, one of fifteen before the election of George Washington, who was the first United States President under the Constitution. Peyton Randolph and his wife had no children; therefore, his nephew, Edmund Randolph, became the heir to the Peyton properties, and he was Minty's master. Minty remembered Edmund Randolph as a kindly man. She had learned that he was famous for being one of the Founding Fathers and one of the most popular figures in Virginia politics. The Constitution had been drawn up with his help, and it was upon his motion that the word *slavery* was omitted from the Constitution. Even though he himself owned many slaves, he advocated prohibiting the importation of slaves. He refused to sell any of his increase because he could not bear separating his Negro families. He, as well as other Randolphs, realized the importance of keeping their slaves content and hard working. They believed that a married slave made for a good slave. This led to the reproduction of more slaves, and it made the slaves become tied down and less likely to run away. Also, good housing and adequate food provision kept their slaves content. Hard working slaves were often rewarded by being put in charge of other slaves.

The Randolph slaves were referred to as "Randies". However, many of them did not keep the name of Randolph, even though it was customary for slaves to keep the name of a present owner or a previous owner. Later, this helped the freed slaves in reuniting with separated families and other relatives who had been cruelly torn apart. Might Minty have somehow reestablished a relationship with her family? One can only wonder.

Through the years at the Randolph plantation Minty learned much more about her master. He had been an aide de camp to George Washington in the Revolutionary War, an Attorney General, the Governor of Virginia, and he had been entirely entrusted with the business affairs in Virginia of the president. After his uncle died in 1775, he became the heir to 7,000 acres of land, several houses, and about 200 slaves.

As Minty had continued growing up in the Randolph home, she most likely followed her mother around the household, do-ing little tasks, all the while learn-ing what was to be expected of her. She may well have watched her mother seeing to the comfort of the visiting dig-nitaries. Some-times Minty played with the Randolph chil-dren, Edmonia and Lucy, who were her age, and Susan who was a few years older. Peyton thought he was too old to be bothered with the young ones.

Family of Edmund Randolph

Peyton Randolph 1721-1775

Edmund Randolph 1753-1813

1) Peyton Randolph (1779-1828)

2) Susan Randolph Taylor (1781-1846)

3) Edmonia Randolph Preston (1787-1847)

4) Lucy Randolph Daniel (1789-)

From time to time Minty often heard the Randolph children repeat things they had heard their father say. One thing she remembered was his saying that "Woman, in the present state of society, without religion, is a monster." Another was that "the good of man consisted in Christianity alone." (From Old Churches, Ministers, and Families of Virginia)

At the time that Minty was born, trouble was brewing as to the slavery issue, an issue that those acting as delegates to the Constitutional Convention would rather avoid. Some states wanted to continue importing slaves, while others wanted slavery to be abolished. A dilemma. Little sympathy was extended toward those advocating freedom for their slaves.

Although Minty understood little of what was being said at the time, she gathered that many of the Founding Fathers wanted to see slavery abolished, but in the South, where slavery was the backbone of agriculture, states could have walked out and formed their own nation. The cultivation of rice, cotton, and tobacco required slaves to work from dawn to dusk. At the Convention, those in favor of slavery wanted their slaves to be part of their population count, whereas, opponents of slavery wanted slave trade abolished. A compromise was reached wherein three out of every five slaves could be counted. In Article 1, Section 9 of the Constitution, the Fugitive Slave Clause required a state to which an escapee fled to return that slave to his owner in another state.

At this point in Minty's life, these changes had little effect upon her; however, many of her fellow human beings did suffer as a result. She would much later hear tell of many such sufferings such as one related by Levi Coffin, the president of the Underground Railroad. He told of seeing a slave owner who had been notified that his runaway slave had been lodged in jail and that he could be picked up. When asked by his owner why he had run away after being treated kindly, the captured slave replied, "My wife and children were taken away from me, and I think as much of them as you do of yours, or any white man does of his. Their massa tried to buy me, too, but you would not sell me, so when I saw them go away, I followed."

The master said, "I've always treated you well, trusting you with my keys, and treating you more like a confidential servant than a slave, but now you shall know what slavery is. Just wait till I get you home."

Irons were put on the captured slave and a chain was riveted around his neck, and handcuffs on his wrists. Laying the Negro's fettered hand on an anvil, his owner struck it with a hammer until blood settled under the finger nails. A chain was fastened to the Negro's neck and to the axle of the wagon. As the wagon disappeared from sight, the poor man was running to keep up with the wagon. (Taken from Reminiscences of Levi Coffin, the Reputed President of the Underground Railroad, by Levi Coffin, Biblio Bazaar, LLC.)

Although at the time Minty heard about or witnessed such happenings, she didn't understand the situations, but later her heart ached as she recalled these events.

Chapter Three

Minty,
a Slave, Yet Not a Slave

Smiles crept across Minty's face whenever childhood memories came to her mind. Until Minty reached the age of six or seven, she, like many slave children, had no idea that she was a slave, or that she was different from the white Randolph children with whom she was a playmate.

One of the duties of a slave child often was to be a playmate to the master's children. Living within the mansion house with her mother, Minty felt on the same level, especially with Edmonia and Lucy. Minty, like all children, loved to play. She even had some of the cherished castoff toys, such as some homemade marbles, broken dolls, or a tattered ball, much like those that have been found in slave cabins. Never a new toy.

Sometimes in their playtime, the young Minty and the other children played *Bob the Needle*. In this game, they used a needle case. They would circle up, with one child in the center.

While singing a song, the children in the circle would pass the needle case behind their backs. When the song was over, the child in the middle had to guess who had the needle case. [Our version, *Button, Button, Who's got the Button?*]

Broken toys

Another game loved by Minty and her playmates was *Miss Mary Mack*. This fun rhyme was actually a game that the children played to make fun of the Master's daughter. The toys in this game were their own hands, and as they played they chanted the ditty. The point of the song was how silly the

Children playing Bob the Needle

master's daughter was for spending money to see an elephant jump over a fence, because everyone knew an elephant could not jump a fence.

A bath time game was *Here We Go Loopty Loo*. This popular song required children to put their right hand in, put their right hand out and give their hand a shake. Then they moved on to the left hand, the right foot, and so on. This song helped to describe bath time on a slave plantation. Water from a local stream had to be heated by fire in a large washtub that sat outside. The Mammy, or the slave who ran the childcare on the plantation, was in charge of bath time, and had to get every child bathed quickly. So as they sang, the children would gather around the bath tub and go through the motions described in the song as they bathed together.

Minty never learned to read or write since, with few exceptions, slave children were not allowed to be educated. Still, they learned to count from the master's children while playing such games as hide and seek. Minty's education came from what she heard from others and what she witnessed or experienced. Games of guessing riddles were a challenge to her intellect. Two such riddles are listed below:

Slick as a mole, black as coal.
Got a great long tail like a thunder hole.
(Skillet)

Crooked as a rainbow, teeth like a cat,
Guess all of your life, but you can't guess that.
(Blackberry bush)

The games enjoyed by Minty and her playmates were not much different than those played by children today. And for the time being, Minty's world, in her estimation, was no different than her white playmates. However, this would soon change.

Chapter Four

Slave Ships (Minty Learns About Her Ancestors)

Filling up her basket with pieces of driftwood as she shuffled along the shoreline of the Ohio River, Minty often recalled the few free times she spent sharing her tales of the white man's world with her mother and other black household members, or listening to their tales. Some of these tales included the background of slaves, tales of how their own ancestors had become slaves. Minty knew very little about her ancestry, but what little she did know was gleaned from the tales told by her parents, tales overheard from among

From Slave Trade Collection, Virginia, edu.

the older slaves, or conversations between visitors on the plantation.

As Minty grew older the bits of information fit together piece by piece in puzzle-like fashion. At first Minty was confused with the talk about slaves, but one day she realized that she, too, was a slave. She learned that black Africans were often captured by men they had never seen before, and some even captured by their own tribal leaders. They then were sold, put on ships, and set to sea.

Minty could not imagine the grief and agony these poor souls suffered. Oh, the tears that must have flowed! Tears! Tears for those left behind! Tears for being snatched away from home and loved ones! No idea where they were going or if they would ever return. They were bound in chains. Screaming did no good. No one was listening. They were yelled at! Beaten! They didn't understand the strange language. Their eyes filled with fright! Tears covered their cheeks! The filth! The stench! The crowded, cramped space! Stowed away on a ship that would be their home for the next thirty to fifty days!

As Minty began to understand these tales of terror, she realized that some of these black Africans could have been her ancestors. They were no longer treated as human beings. They were mere objects of trade, worth about one hundred and fifty dollars each. Minty was curious as to why this happened to them. As she listened she learned that cheap labor was needed to work the plantations, and this made slave-trading a profitable business, more valuable than the trading for goods, such as spices and gold.

Minty probably heard tell of one ship, the Brookes. It had been discovered to have carried

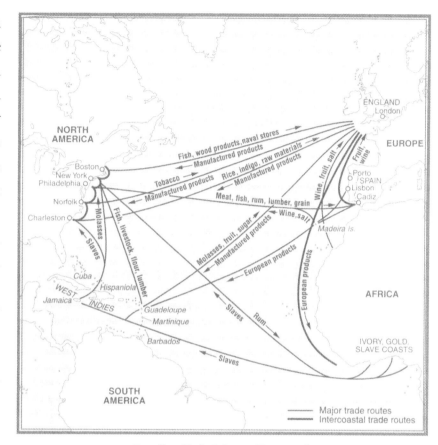

From Slave Trade Collection, Virginia, edu.

over six hundred slaves when built to only carry a maximum of four hundred and fifty-two. On these ships the slaves would be chained together by their hands and feet with little room to move. They were packed together like "books on a shelf", with only four feet or so of head room.

The captured blacks were branded with red-hot irons, either under their breasts or on their arms, just like cattle. Sometimes these poor human beings had to sit between each other's legs and were placed so close together that they could not lie down, nor

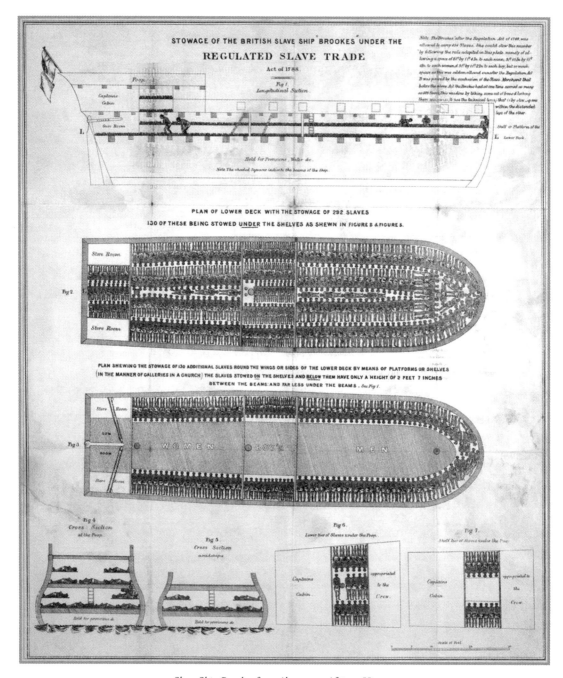

Slave Ship Brookes from About.com African History

could they change their position. Little air and light made its way into the hold, and the heat was suffocating.

Sickness and even death attacked the "cargo" confined in that filthy foul smelling place. Hungry sharks followed the ships, waiting for those that died of dysentery and other complaints. The waiting owners on the other side of the world would be fortunate to receive half their goods.

The illustration on the previous page gives a detailed drawing of the slave ship Brookes, showing how four hundred and eighty-two people were to be packed onto the decks. The detailed plans and cross sectional drawing of the slave ship Brookes was distributed by the Abolitionist Society in England as part of their campaign against the slave trade, and dates from 1789. [From About.com African History]

All necessities for a healthy supply of cargo caused constant problems on the voyages. The scarce supply of food consisted of rice, beans, yams, palm oil, and a little water. Bodily needs were met with buckets and sometimes a washing down by crew members. For warmth at night, ragged shirts and pants were the only blankets. The hot humid air and filth on the floor made for poor sanitation. As for exercise, this was determined by weather conditions. In good weather, women and children were sometimes allowed to move around on the ship's deck during the day. The men's exercise consisted of a shuffling dance performed on deck while cruel crew members snapped whips at their naked bodies.

Because of the close quarters, poor sanitation, hygiene, and food supply, disease was easily transmitted on the slave ships. The flux, smallpox, and scurvy were the most common killers, leaving the ship decks often covered with blood and mucus. Up to twenty-five percent of the cargo of slaves died and were dumped overboard. Most fearful of the diseases was that which affected the eyes. This often led to blindness. The disease,

Slaves on the Dutch HMS Daphne

known as ophthalmia, was caused by the intense heat, the glare of the sun, a strong wind which carried dust, and poor sanitation. The affected eye would swell, become inflamed, fill with mucus, and become stuck shut. Soon the vision would be disturbed, and then complete blindness. The barely trained doctors on slave ships were unable to handle the many cases of the various diseases. Their main treatment was that of "bleeding".

Many of the slaves attempted suicide. They believed that their death would return them to their homeland and to their friends and relatives. To keep the slaves from killing themselves, sailors chopped the heads off corpses, and said that when they died, they would return home headless. Some of the slaves even died of broken hearts.

Grisly tools of bondage

A discovered photo shows East African slaves taken aboard the Dutch HMS Daphne on the Indian Ocean from an Arab dhow, on November 1, 1868. This group of severely emaciated boys and young men on the lower deck of a Royal Naval ship apparently had been taken from what was a slave vessel trading illegally off the African coast headed to the Americas. The captain of the Royal Naval ship had instructions not to return the rescued slaves to the place on the coast where they had been put on the slave ship, probably because they were in danger of being recaptured.

Discoveries on slave ships have revealed the basics required by slave traders: iron bars, glass beads and pewter ware to trade for humans in Africa; linen and calico cloth, indigo and paint for the British inhabitants of the Caribbean, where the slaves would eventually be sold; weapons, fresh water, tobacco, rum, and brandy and wine for the crew.

And, of course, the grisly tools of bondage: heavy chains, iron collars and shackles for slaves' necks, wrists and ankles, and sharp contraptions to pry open the mouths of African men and women who attempted to defy their fate by starving themselves. Note the irons even for babies. (These pictures were posted by Michael Cottman, political writer for the Washington Post, February 7, 1999.)

Advertisement typical of the times

When the putrid smelling cargo ships, covered with swarming flies, entered the bustling port, the slaves that were still alive were unloaded and herded into holding pens where they remained until the sale. Palm oil was rubbed on their skin to make it look brighter. The sickly looking slaves were sold for a cheap price, and the buyers had hopes of getting a better price if these regained their health. All of these things Minty had overheard over the years. It was difficult for Minty, who had never seen a huge ship or great body of water, to visualize these things. However, she would be able to relate to the cruelties afflicted upon slaves. Over time, she had witnessed for herself, afflictions seen at slave sales, whippings, and families being torn apart. Might her own ancestors have suffered these same tortures? Visions of these oft-told mournful tales remained with Minty for the rest of her life.

Chapter Five

Minty's Young Childhood

Minty, however, didn't spend much time thinking about her captured ancestors. Nor did she think about what was going on in the outside world. She was kept busy, whether playing with the master's children or taking care of the usual daily tasks around the mansion such as dusting, pulling weeds, feeding chickens, gathering eggs, chasing geese out of the yard, fanning flies from the owner's table, taking lunch to the master's children at school, and running various errands. Sometimes she would be taken on excursions with her mistress to visit a neighbor, and all the while she was absorbing the things which would make her the valuable domestic she would become, a domestic who needed to know the customs of the elite. During Minty's time off from work, she had the freedom, to some extent, to pursue her own interests and exercise some measure of control over her own life. She spent this time in anything but being idle.

Even though she had to be available whenever the Master or Mistress requested, Minty shared in the many ways to fill the "free" hours with her family. Each free evening, on Sundays, and on the occasional holidays, she busied herself with activities for her family's benefit. Most important on a daily basis was her "housekeeping" chores, such as tending chickens and garden plots, cooking and preserving the produce of these gardens, and caring for clothing of the family. Other "after hours" activities enabled a slave family to earn money, which was then used to buy small luxuries and thus raise their standard of living, possibly better clothing, extra food, and household goods.

For entertainment Minty found the singing with other slaves and listening to tales of things that came from Africa especially enjoyable.

Negro spirituals, which were called "corn ditties", and folk songs, were favorites during their gatherings, especially on Saturday and Sunday evenings, at various homes in the slave quarters. One of their favorites was "Sweet Canaan, the Promised Land".

Some of the African American religious singing at this time was referred to as a "moan" or a "groan". Moaning, or groaning, does not imply pain. It is a kind of blissful rendition of a song, often mixed with humming and spontaneous melodic variation.

Minty especially enjoyed the fun songs. One much later old fashioned ballad is an example typical of their fun songs.

Jeff Davis rode a big white horse, but Lincoln rode a mule—
Jeff Davis was a fine, smart man, and Lincoln was a fool.
Jeff Davis had a fine white; Lincoln only had a mule—
Jeff Davis was a wonderful man and Lincoln was a fool.

The slaves loved their music, and the banjo and guitar, usually home-made, were their musical instruments. Depending upon the place and custom, banjoes were constructed by different materials. To make a fairly good fiddle, all a skilled craftsman needed was a good knife, some boards, and gut from a slaughtered cow that had been gutted. This gut was dried and carefully cut into strips. Some fiddles were made of gourds and strings and bows of horsehair. A banjo might be made from half a fruit with a very hard rind, such as a calabash or a gourd, by stretching a piece of thin skin or piece of bladder, over the opening, adding two or three strings made from gut and raising the string on a bridge. Or it could be made by stretching the tanned hide of a woodchuck or groundhog over a piece of timber fashioned like a cheese box.

Uncle Tom's Cabin.   Onkel Toms Hütte.

Playin' on the old banjo

Sometimes the bowl of the gourd was not cut away and the instrument had the appearance of a mandolin.

For other kinds of instruments, the slaves used any and all kinds of material that could be forced to make a musical sound — old pieces of iron, ribs of sheep, jawbone of cows or horses, pieces of wood and sticks. When in the absence of musical instruments for creating sound and rhythm, the slaves often used "patting", striking the hands on the knees, then striking the hands together, then striking the right shoulder with one hand, the left with the other—all the time keeping time with the feet. Another means was by striking the cupped hand or palm of hand or fingers over the mouth of a jug or big bottle. Recalling these "fun times", often changed a frown to a smile on Minty's wrinkled face.

The slaves had their "work songs", their "quiet songs", and their "secret message songs", as well as their religious songs. Their songs were linked with their lives as slaves. The work songs dealt with their daily life, and the spirituals were inspired by the message of Jesus Christ and his Gospel. These songs indicated the hard conditions of the life of a slave. They expressed feelings of sadness and heartache, longing for freedom, and sometimes attempts at cheering one another. Many of the slaves tried to run to a "free country" that they called "my home" or "Sweet Canaan, the Promised Land". The country was on the northern side of the Ohio River which was called "Jordan". Some of their songs referred to the Underground Railroad and were used as signals to indicate danger or safety.

Some of these included:

Wade in the Water

Wade in the water,
Wade in the water children.
Wade in the water

God's gonna trouble the water

The Gospel Train

The Gospel train's comin'
I hear it just at hand
I hear the car wheel rumblin'
and rollin' thro' the land

Get on board little children
Get on board little children
Get on board little children
there's room for many more

Swing Low, Sweet Chariot

Swing low, sweet chariot
coming for to carry me home...

Another activity Minty found enjoyable in her younger days was watching the older slaves who were also very fond of sports. One of the most common was hurdle racing. Here, the contestants would leap over hurdles placed at regular intervals apart. A similar game was that of leaping over a high hurdle using a small pole about twelve feet in length.

Perhaps the favorite contest was called "A Free for all". Here a ring was drawn on the ground which ranged from about fifteen feet to thirty feet in diameter, depending on the number of contestants who engaged in the combat. Each participant was given a kind of bag that was stuffed with cotton and rags into a very compact mass. When so stuffed, each bag would weigh on an average of ten pounds and was used by the contestant in striking his antagonist. Each combatant picked whichever opponent he desired and attempted to subdue him by pounding him over the head with the bag which he used as his weapon of defense or which was used as an offensive weapon. The contest would continue in this manner till every combatant was counted out and a hero of the contest proclaimed. Sometimes two contestants were adjudged heroes, and it was necessary to run a contest between the two combatants before a final hero could be proclaimed. Then the two antagonists would stage a battle royal and would continue in the conflict till one was proclaimed victorious.

Sometimes these free-for-all battles were carried on with a kind of improvised boxing gloves, and the contests were carried on in the same manner as previously described. Minty and her friends looked forward to the time when they could participate in these adult sports, and sometimes they tried their own childish versions of these.

This was Minty's world, but during this time of her young childhood, much was taking place outside in another world. When she was four years old, an inventor by the name of Eli Whitney, invented the cotton gin, making cotton more profitable. Also, the First Fugitive Slave Law had passed, allowing slave owners to cross state lines in the pursuit of their runaways and making it a penal offense to aid the runaway slaves. Slave trade between the U.S, and foreign countries was prohibited at this time. These things had no meaning for a young Minty.

Life on the Randolph plantation molded Minty's character into that which would be witnessed in her for years to come.

Chapter Six

A New Chapter for
Minty

Sometimes Minty's mind traveled back to the time of her first separation, and as she slowly stooped to grasp a dropped sliver of wood, tears trickled down her cheeks. She could still feel the warmth of her mother's last hug and hear her words of comfort. Her thoughts drifted to the events which led up to this separation.

At the time of Washington's death, Minty had reached the age where she had become part of a group called "working boys and girls". This ended her period of relative freedom. Prior to this time, while parents were doing chores in the big house, children were left alone to raise each other. Minty, as well as others, was kept busy with the multitude of small tasks around the plantation house and lawns, and always at the beck and call of the older slaves.

Now that she had become a "working girl", her responsibilities changed to more arduous domestic tasks, such as spinning thread, weaving cloth, turning tallow into soap, dipping candles, washing laundry, and cooking food. Her new tasks prepared her to step into any home as a well- rounded domestic. A young slave girl never knew when she might be "loaned out" to someone in need.

Minty knew that young slave girls were often given to the master's young daughter as a birthday or wedding gift to become her

Miss Susan

personal slave. She often pondered about whom she might be given to. Sometimes she imagined what it would be like to have to be leaving her family.

She didn't have to wait long because she was soon given to one of the three Randolph daughters as a birthday gift. Randolph's daughter, Miss Susan, who was seven years older than Minty, became her "young mistress". She already loved Miss Susan whom she thought to be the prettiest girl she had ever seen.

Minty's duties had again completely changed. Now she was constantly at the beck and call of her new mistress, whatever Miss Susan's whim

Typical bridal gown for the period

might be. She slept on a pallet in the same room as her young mistress so as to be near if she had any needs during the night, a drink of water, a fanning to cool her, or a cool cloth to soothe a headache. She had to quietly arise before her mistress awoke and gently stir the coals and add firewood to the fireplace to make the room toasty warm in chilly weather. Then, fresh clothing for the day must be laid out. After helping her young mistress dress, Minty carefully brushed and arranged the curly locks to satisfy her.

Minty accompanied Miss Susan to the dining area, standing nearby to make sure everything was satisfactory. Many times she would have to listen to the constant giggles and chatter of Susan and her visiting friends or little sisters while also attending to their needs. This could be tiresome because it was customary for visitors to stay as guests for several days at a time. As a reward for her attention, Minty might sometimes be given an unwanted or broken piece of jewelry as a reward.

Time passed, and suddenly, one year after Washington's death, Minty's world as she had known it crashed! Miss Susan had recently married John Bennett Taylor. The year was 1801. Minty had been right in the middle of all the frustrations brought on with preparations. She even helped with sewing the wedding dress. How her eyes had filled with tears as she watched Miss Susan dressing for the ceremony. The elegant wedding celebration had been an exciting time for Minty. She thought that her mistress was the most beautiful bride ever.

White roses, white orchids, lilies of the valley, and orange blossoms had filled every vacant space as well as having been carried by the bridesmaids.

As was customary, the Randolphs had invited their household slaves to enjoy the wedding festivities; however, they were set apart from the other guests. The reception after had left wonderful memories for Minty. The dancing, the games, and the heavenly aroma and sight of the luscious food. Ham, oysters, enormous roasts of beef and pork, jams, jellies, spirited punches and toddies, quivery desserts, cakes, and pies filled with fruit and cream.

During the wedding and reception after, the slaves had been free from having to attend to the needs and wants of the guests who filled the elegant guest rooms. They watched from a distance as the guests congratulated the groom. The bride was never congratulated, since it was considered poor etiquette.

Minty's exhilaration was short lived. As a child, innocently unaware of the possibilities of separation, she was soon to learn of the pain that separation could cost. She overheard the sly whispers and quiet conversations among the household slaves; something about her being taken away from the only home she had ever known. Little did Minty know what was in store for her, the life changing adventure she would soon be experiencing, one that would bring a myriad of new characters across the stage of her life. Not only had a tearful Minty witnessed the loss of her Master's beloved friend, George Washington, but now she was soon to be cruelly torn from the only home she had ever known and her own family whom she dearly loved. As a frightened Minty dutifully went about her daily chores, she continued to overhear more confusing comments. She was to be taken on a long journey with her "young mistress" to some faraway place called Kentucky.

The Taylors were going to Kentucky for a honeymoon, a custom which had become quite fashionable for the elite. It was also fashionable for

Minty could have traveled to Kentucky in a coach like this.

wealthy families to visit the popular mineral springs near Lexington, Kentucky.

In fact, Susan's best friend, recently married Nellie Parke Custis Washington, had spent her honeymoon at one of the springs in Kentucky. Minty overheard them talking about one particular spring that had a hotel with a dining room which could cater to one hundred ladies and gentlemen and cabins for families who preferred to board themselves. Many were the social activities provided. The famous Olympian Springs was advertised in April of 1805 for its "most pure and salubrious air, romantic and picturesque scenery, the best music, dancing, bathing, swinging, riding, and hunting." Barbeques were also in fashion, and public dinners were given every other Thursday in Lexington.

Minty was soon told that the rumors of her being separated from her family and friends were true. A woeful young black slave girl helped her mistress pack several trunks, and one day an elegant stage coach drawn by beautiful horses pulled up in front of the plantation's mansion. Thirteen year old Minty, dressed in her finest, and her eighteen year old Mistress Susan were bundled into the coach, their belongings stashed upon the roof of the coach, and as the four prancing horses, anxious to get on their way, strained at their load, Minty waved at the tearful group of slaves in the background bidding her a forever farewell. While not wanting to disturb her mistress, she continued to take cautious looks backward until her loved ones, especially her mother with her white apron held up to her eyes, were no longer in sight.

Through tear-filled eyes and between muffled sobs, Minty gazed upon the landscape all around her, indelibly painting a picture in her mind to be called up whenever she became homesick. She dare not express her feelings of despair, because as a slave, she was forbidden to show sorrowful emotions that might cause discomfort to Miss Susan or the other travelers.

Minty bounced and jounced as the stage jostled along the bumpy trail leading to this strange place called Kentucky. Every twelve miles the stage came to a jolting halt and fresh horses replaced the tired steeds. Weary and dusty travelers climbed slowly down from the stage and stretched their stiff legs, refreshed themselves, and hungrily ate a bowl of soup or stew provided by the hostler at the relay station. A flutter of excitement always arose as the stage sped along the rough trail at top speed. The stage did not often travel at high speed though because much of the road was not much more than a trail. It was kept clear of brush and stumps by the settlers who had the responsibility of keeping the road which ran through their property passable. In some places the road was covered with crushed stone and in others with wooden planks. However, none of the excitement took away the fighting back of tears, nor the unrelenting ache in Minty's heart. Her young mistress told her they would be going to a place called the Clermont Plantation, owned by Green Clay. A tired and lonely little slave girl yearned to be back home.

The beginning of Minty's adventure had introduced her to what was to become the National Road. Even though much of what the passengers said was confusing, she listened with interest as the other travelers discussed its construction. Part of the road was first known as "Boone's Trace". The Transylvania Company had sent Daniel Boone with thirty men to hack a trail into the lush valleys beyond the mountains. In less than three weeks, Boone's men blazed a trail of two hundred eight miles through the Cumberland Gap, which is five hundred ten miles from Washington, D.C., and into what is now Kentucky.

This painting exhibits how the road was cleared.

The road made a long loop from Virginia southward to Tennessee and then northward into Kentucky. Only on June 1, 1792, after Kentucky had become a state, was the trail wide enough for wagons. The road had been made by chopping out underbrush and small trees in a swath only ten to thirty feet wide and cutting off the larger timber eighteen inches from the ground.

The axe men had to leave the largest trees standing, some even in the middle of the road. They bridged small streams with logs, and crossed rivers by fords or ferries. Even under the best conditions such roads were unsatisfactory, and during wet weather they were impassable.

The Wilderness Road

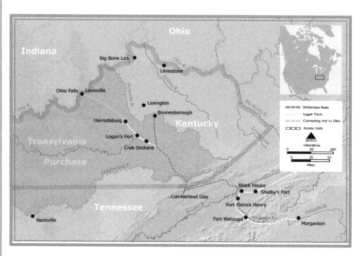

Map of the Wilderness Road to Kentucky

Front and back of Whitehall which was built around the original house built by Green Clay, a small two story structure called Clermont

Nevertheless, they connected the East to the West, and that was enough.

After many uncomfortable and boring days of seeing nothing but trees, trees, and more trees, rivers, some almost uncrossable, and much wildlife, Minty was nearing the end of what had been a wearisome journey. The stage slowed and she saw before her what was to become her home for the next twenty years or so.

Minty, a thirteen-years-old slave girl, was about to begin the first page of this new chapter in her life. What a surprise awaited her!

Chapter Seven

A Change for Minty:
Slave Breeding

Minty soon learned another possible reason for this trip to Kentucky and why she had been brought to this place. She was loaned out to General Green Clay and was to be married to one of his slaves, his personal valet, Lewis O'Banion. Had a deal been made with the new Mrs. Taylor to introduce a new bloodline into the slave population on the Green Plantation with this marriage? Had Minty been married to Lewis O'Banion for the purpose of being a part of a new crop, the breeding of slaves, a highly profitable practice for slave owners in the states of Virginia, Kentucky, and Tennessee?

Minty's former owner, Edmund Randolph, and new owner, Green Clay, were both highly involved in the political world of Virginia and in the economical world of slavery where this type of trading of slaves for the purpose of gaining more slaves was frequent.

A frightened Minty wondered who this Lewis O'Banion was. Since his last name was O'Banion, he evidently had been a slave to one of the O'Banion slave holding families in Kentucky, and had been purchased by General Green Clay. [Census records show O'Banion slave owners in Shelby, Washington, and Garrard Counties in Kentucky.] Since Lewis was Clay's valet, he must have been trustworthy.

Little did Minty realize what this practice of slave breeding involved for her. As time went on and she went about her domestic duties, she overheard many conversations taking place among the frequent visitors at Whitehall. Also, she was enlightened by her husband, Lewis. She soon understood that since Kentucky was not suitable for raising cotton because of the hilly ground, few field slaves were needed for the common crop of hemp. However, the southern states had great need for field slaves. The rapid expansion of cotton, tobacco, sugar cane, and rice production in the Deep South called for more labor. Those who were against slavery, while still owning slaves themselves, foresaw a banning of the slave trade and were simply trying to get more slaves. , [This banning did take place in 1808 when the Trans Atlantic slave trade was officially abolished.] Therefore, many landowners, including Thomas Jefferson, had realized the value of "raising their own crop" of slaves to be sold to the South.

Minty recalled having heard about Jefferson expressing his views in two letters of the importance of enslaved women as breeders. He stated,

A coffle

"Their value is not in their work, but in the number of children they will have and nurture to a productive age. Women need to be given time to care for their children so that ultimately the slaveholder's property will increase." He also wrote: "A child raised every two years is of more profit than the crop of the best laboring man … what she produces is an addition to capital." She knew that it was common for a newborn to be worth two hundred dollars the moment it drew its first breath. In fact, The Plantation Manual advised readers to encourage reproduction by giving every woman with "six children alive" all their Saturdays off. Someone said that one plantation owner, a Major Wallon, offered every new mother a calico dress and a silver dollar. More important than the presents given to many young women was the fact that if they became pregnant, they were much less likely to be sold away from husbands and relatives. Is it any wonder that Minty would be an asset to Green Clay?

Having been a slave for the Randolphs, Minty was

A slave pen for slaves in Alexandria, Virginia,

aware that slave women usually started bearing children around age thirteen. By age twenty, they would likely have had four or five. Some slave women might have twenty or more children in their lifetime. She had heard that in order to encourage child bearing some plantation

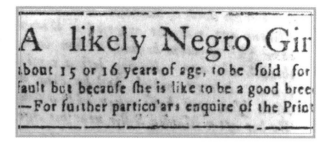

Examples of advertisements for sale of slaves

owners promised their women slaves their freedom after they had produced fifteen children. The slave woman seemed to count every baby born as a "gift from heaven", one step closer to freedom. Young women were often advertised for sale as "good breeding stock", as the these advertisements indicates. Many slave dealers kept an eye out for advertisements that might hint at possible "breeders".

Between 1820 and 1860 more than 60 percent of the Upper South's enslaved population were "sold South," and Mississippi's enslaved population alone increased by more than 225 percent. Once slaves were bought by slave traders, whether men, women, or children, they were put into iron- barred pens called "jails." There they waited until they were either loaded onto steamboats and transported by river or chained hand and foot in a column of two's forming a caravan called a coffle and marched 25-30 miles a day down a series of trails known as the Natchez Trace, into the Deep South. Arriving in Natchez, they were put into holding pens to await purchase. Virginia alone exported between six thousand and fifteen

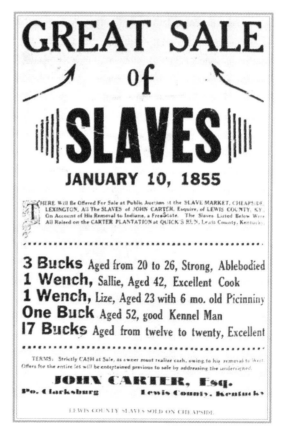

thousand slaves a year in the early decades of the nineteenth century, causing Thomas Dew, a professor at William and Mary College, to proclaim it "a Negro raising state for other states".

One slave trader from Virginia boasted that his successful breeding policies enabled him to sell six thousand slave children a year. One slave dealer in Lexington, Kentucky advertised in 1853 that he was offering twelve hundred to twelve hundred and fifty dollars for slaves to be carried to the New Orleans Market. Traders kept an eye out for advertisements of slaves for sale.

One might wonder why the churches did not speak out against this practice of slave breeding.

Minty, indeed, was about to become an asset to Green Clay's slave production. She was overcome with the fear of what lay ahead for her. Would she be separated from her future offspring? Would they, too, be advertised and sold to the South? Would someone else be snuggling her little ones?

A painting of a Mammy and her snuggling charges

Chapter Eight

Minty's New Master,

Green Clay

O ften Minty's thoughts would bring recollections of the years spent on the Clermont plantation and what she had discovered about its owner and his family. Who was this man?

His name was Green Clay, later known as General Green Clay. He was a senator and orator of that time. Green Clay had fought in the Revolutionary War under George Washington and had become one of Madison County's most influential citizens in the county's early history. He held many political offices for Madison County, Kentucky at the same time that Edmund Randolph was Governor of Virginia. Both of these men spent time in Williamsburg, Virginia and were well-acquainted, as the Randolphs did much entertaining.

Green Clay was believed to be the wealthiest man in Kentucky. He owned the most land and the most slaves in the state, having gained the property from the government by being a surveyor in this new territory which would soon become a state separate from Virginia. He received half of all the land he surveyed. [In Clay's will, he lists by name 91 slaves, with their increase, to be given to his children.]

His vast empire included forty thousand acres of farm land,

Jumping the broom.

gristmills, brick kilns, lumber mills, distilleries, taverns, tobacco, slaves, ferries, a toll road, two large warehouses, and a spa resort called Estill Springs. The Estill Springs Resort was a popular vacation spot. Clay ran an advertisement describing the accommodations as being new, large, and well furnished and located one-half mile from where all the leading roads to the upper country (Eastern Kentucky) intersected.

When Minty arrived at Clermont, and put to work as a domestic, the Clay family had two children of their own. Soon after her arrival, she and Lewis O'Banion "jumped the broom". A broom was placed in front of each of them. Each then stepped over his/her broom and joined hands to signal they were truly married. To be more festive, the couple may have each jumped backward over a broom held a foot from the ground. If either one failed to clear the broom successfully, the other partner would be declared the one who would rule or boss the household. If both partners cleared the broom without touching it, then there would be no "bossin".

This method of "jumping the broom" was considered by most as a binding force.

As was customary for a slave girl of twelve or thirteen years old to have reached the child-bearing age, Minty commenced at once to be productive. She would be at the Clay Plantation for almost twenty years and during this time be the producer of nine or ten children. When Lewis and Minty were set free, eight of their children had to remain as slaves to General Clay since the offspring of slaves belonged to the Master. [Ohio census records for 1830 show a daughter between the ages of ten and twenty-four and two sons under ten. The daughter would have been born in Kentucky and redeemed, and the two sons would have been born in Ohio.]

Life for Minty on the Clay plantation was that of a domestic, and Lewis was Clay's personal valet. As valet, Lewis served well. He kept the general's bedroom in order, served his meals with dignity and style, and was always on hand to meet his every need, even accompanying him on his travels. A valet was usually a trusted slave and was given many responsibilities. He would have the keys to the wine cellar, be "at the door", "at the gate", and "at the carriage".

He had special tasks such as managerial and ceremonial responsibilities which included coordinating the activities of front house servants. He must always look well-groomed and was able to travel alone without having a pass.

As a domestic, Minty's duties, aside from producing babies and caring for them, included caring for the Clay offspring. Women slaves were far less genteel and less comfortable than men household slaves. Her duties included that of cooking, building fires, milking cows, preparing breakfast, cleaning, doing laundry outside in boiling pots of water, using lye soap, ironing, preparing meals, making and mending clothes, and tending the sick. Minty had been trained well at the Randolphs.

As Minty's own children were growing up, they had little chores around the house. By the age of four they might be building fires, and by age six, rocking the master's children to sleep for naps. One of her sons had been chosen as a houseboy. His tasks included fetching water, waiting tables, gardening, some household tasks and some outside. He would serve as an inexpensive but convenient laborer around the farmhouse.

The first ten years at the Clay Plantation found Minty with at least six children. Her possible sixth child was born about the same time as the Clay's son Cassius Marcellus (1810). [The boxer, Mohammad Ali, whose actual name was Cassius Clay, was the great, great grandson of a slave set free by Green Clay's son, Cassius Clay. Ali had his name changed because he did not want to be associated with a slave holding family.] Still, Minty's childbearing days were not over.

Minty had many fond memories of her years at the Clay plantation. How could she forget the rascally Cassius Marcellus. How he loved to fight! Then would follow the whipping from his mother with her ever ready peach tree rod. His last whipping followed his running away from his mother with Minty and the other servants chasing after him. He lodged himself upon a stone pile and began pelting them as they tried to take hold of him. Then his mother approached! The stone dropped from his raised hand. A somber Cassius took his last whipping.

Cassius' father was his hero and he loved hearing the tale of Fort Meigs over and over. The only time his father ever struck him was when Cassius teased the Billy goat. The goat was tied to a tree and Cassius would stand just out of reach of a head butting. When the general saw the goat running toward his son with his head bent low, ready to butt, only to be snapped up short, Cassius found himself sprawled upon the ground from his father's blow.

Cassius would later become an anti-slavery crusader and publisher of an abolitionist newspaper, *The American*. He received many death threats and regularly barricaded the armored doors of his newspaper office for protection. He also set up two four-pounder cannons inside. After a mob broke in and destroyed his equipment he set up a publication center in Cincinnati. [Since Minty had helped to raise Cassius, this would have given her opportunity for access to news about her left-behind family in Kentucky.] Clay remained closely connected with the northern abolitionist movement and became a friend of Abraham Lincoln.

Minty smiled as she recalled the many lessons the general taught his children. "Never tell your business to anyone." "Don't trust strangers." "Enquire of fools and children if you wish to get at the truth." "When traveling in dangerous times, never return by the same road." Minty taught many of these wise sayings to her own children.

She recalled that Green Clay had spent much time away from his family because of his political and military positions. Also, he was a man who avoided unnecessary conflicts and provided his slaves with first-class food, clothing, and shelter.

Chapter Nine

Minty and Lewis
Off to War

$\mathcal{M}$inty often recalled that her duties as a slave included more than that of a domestic in the home of her master. As the wife of Clay's valet, she was expected to accompany him whenever he traveled with the master. Green Clay was a powerful and influential man by the time the War of 1812 started, the 32-month military conflict between the United States of America and the United Kingdom of Great Britain and Ireland, its North American colonies, and its Indian allies. Clay was commissioned by Kentucky's first governor and ordered to form a regiment of

Tecumseh Kentucky Militia to defend the western frontier from the British and Indians. When the British and their Indian allies under Chief Tecumseh tried to lay siege to Fort Meigs, Clay and his 1,200 Kentuckians were sent there to relieve the besieged fort. At this time, Clay added the title of General to his honors.

Tecumseh

During the War of 1812, Lewis had to accompany General Clay on numerous military campaigns, to Fort Meigs and on other expeditions, one of which possibly took them as far as Detroit, Michigan. Minty, always one of that military party, traveled with Lewis as his helpmeet. This meant she would have to leave her "chilluns" behind. By this time she had four or five children, the oldest being about ten years old and expected to help with the care of the younger ones.

While on the march, Lewis's duties were to cook for the general, keep his clothes clean, tending wounds and/or illness, fetching water and toiletry necessities, and whatever else the general might expect. He was expected to be at his master's side at all times, holding the reins of his horse while he mounted, rubbing down the horse, and sometimes accompanying the general onto the battlefield. If perchance the general might be killed, Lewis would be expected to take his body home.

Minty soon learned what camp life was all about. Her tasks remained pretty much the same as back at the plantation, except now under very primitive conditions. She watched and learned from the more experienced camp wives, and was on hand to help Lewis with his tasks.

Fort Meigs

Even though life as Minty had known it at home had vanished, life still went on in the camp. She discovered that women still gave birth to new life at inconvenient times, she included. When the troops were absent, the women and children were left to fend for themselves. Many times a tearful Minty saw widows and orphans quickly being made by the dreadful fighting. She noticed that most wives never regretted accompanying their husbands, rather counting it a joy to be with them, and knowing that they were performing their duty. Minty and Lewis lived in their pitched tent, usually by a river, and kept fires going for soldiers to prepare their suppers. She did laundry, usually in a nearby river, made up her husband's bed, and listened as she heard reprimanding of those who neglected the expected chores of laundresses, seamstresses, cooks, nursemaids, and companions. Sometimes she would even be expected to be on the battlefield helping to pass water to the soldiers.

How she longed to be safely back on the plantation with her "chilluns". She recalled how during the War of 1812 she had to be away from her children for

Maps showing location of Fort Meigs

several months. They left in late March to travel to Fort Meigs and were there until September. What a relief it had been when the war ended and they traveled back to the plantation. No more blood curdling cries throughout the night.

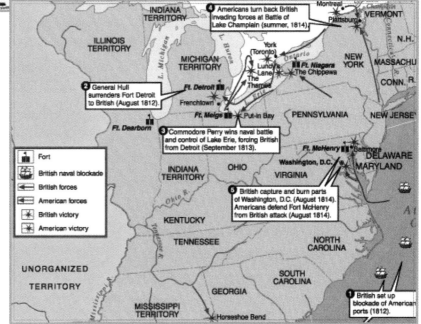

Map showing the War of 1812 battle locations

Chapter Ten

Minty and Lewis
Set Free

As Minty ambled along the shoreline of the Ohio River, searching for washed up scraps of driftwood, the mournful sounds of the steamboat horns matched the mood she had experienced when first coming to Ohio. Sometime after the War of 1812, about 1816 or after when the final treaty was signed, General Clay emancipated Lewis and purchased Minty from her mistress Susan, also emancipating her. What a joyful day that had been! [Remember, the Randolphs did not believe in selling slaves.

Up to this point, although Minty was married to Lewis O'Banion, she had still belonged to her mistress. She must have been leased to Clay.] But then, her joy turned to sadness. The pair were free to leave the Plantation, but where would they go? What would they do? Winslow's painting on the top of page 60 could be Minty, standing in the doorway looking out as conflicting thoughts flooded her mind. "We're free, but what now?"

She and Lewis had their freedom, but didn't know what to do with it. She wondered how they would be accepted out in the white society. They had no home of their own. All of their children born before their emancipation were still slaves of General Green. How could they leave them? The best thing for the time being would be to remain on the Plantation as paid employees and hopefully redeem some of their children.

But would working for white people put them back into slavery again? Would society respect them? Would they respect themselves? Being confused, she and Lewis decided to remain at the Clay Plantation for the time being.

Most frightening of all for Minty was the thought of leaving eight of her children behind. Her oldest child was about eighteen and the youngest a baby. [Lewis and Minty do not show up on the Ohio Census until 1830 with their daughter, between the age of 10-24 and the two sons under 10 living with their father Lewis O'Banion in Chilo Township. The daughter probably had been born free in Kentucky and the boys born in Ohio.]

During this time of indecision for the O'Banions, many from the political world were advocating resettling freed slaves in Africa. The organization of The American Colonization was founded to help resettle these. Also, several states had removed restraints of interstate slave trade, outlawed blacks and mulattos from meeting for the purposes of education, and forbade teaching them to read and write. The United States declared slave trading a capital offense and Canada denied the American Government the right to pursue runaway slaves within its borders. The U.S. annexed East Florida which had been a refuge for runaway slaves. Although Minty and Lewis were not affected by these actions, Florida ceased to be a safe haven and Canada became the future "Promise Land" for runaways.

When the opportunity arose to move to a free state and become employed as a domestic for the Jesse Grant family, the O'Banions agreed. How Minty remembered that sad day of separation. Eight weeping "chilluns" clung to their parents, begging them not to leave. Minty's heart wrenched with pain as memories of a similar day crossed her mind, the day of separation from her mother. How could she leave her babies behind and how could she refuse leaving slavery behind. Minty's tears were tears of joy for freedom, but terrible tears of sorrow at leaving and being wrenched from her beloved "chilluns"! Hope of earning money enough to redeem them fortified her courage.

The pair, with the one child born free, were to be escorted to the Ohio River crossing at Maysville where they would board a steamboat which would drop them off at Point Pleasant, Ohio, a small town on the north side of the river.

After leaving the Clay Plantation, their coach stopped over for the night at Lexington, twenty-five miles to the north of Madison. Lexington was the center for slave auctions in Kentucky. These were held at the Cheapside Auction Block on the public square. Thousands of slaves, bred and raised in Kentucky, were sold here and sent to the South, including children who were separated from their parents.

When they continued on the remaining sixty-six mile journey to the Ohio River the next day, they passed through the square where a slave auction was in progress. The heart wrenching scene brought tears to

Minty's eyes and she choked back sobs. The slaves were made to stand on the auction block while prospective buyers examined them by pulling their mouths open to see their teeth, pinching their arms and legs to see how muscular they were, walking them up and down to see if there were any signs of lameness, making them stoop and bend in different ways to make sure there were no concealed ruptures or wounds, and asking questions as to their qualifications. A young mother clutched her child to her breast. Tears ran down her cheeks as she pleaded that she not be separated from her family. This didn't seem to have any effect on the many speculators who were only interested in adding to their inventory to be sold to the South. A chill ran up her back. Might not some of her own be standing on this very block soon?

1850's drawing of auction block for sale of slaves

Minty had to take her eyes away from the scene before her. How she longed to hold her own little ones in her arms. Would she ever see them again? Would they be sold

Minty may have ridden on a steamboat like this.

on this same auction block? Would they cry at night, longing for her? Minty's heart went out to all those families being torn away from each other all over the slave holding states each year. She would later hear tell of her first master, Edmund Randolph, speaking to the Virginia House of Delegates in 1830, saying that each year for the past twenty years the state of Virginia had sent an average of eight thousand five hundred slaves to the South. (American Slavery As It Is, p. 182.)

Minty had been anxious to leave this heart rending scene of the slave auction, grateful to travel on to a bustling Maysville where they boarded a crowded steamboat.

That trip had been a new experience for Minty. She could still hear the sounds and feel the motions of the boat as it slowly chugged its way along the Ohio River. She had listened as the darkies working on the boat sang their mournful melodies. The rhythmic movement of the boat added to the empty feeling creeping through her insides. Her thoughts had drifted. "Were they lonesome and grieving, too?"

She recalled seeing a gentleman who had purchased several Negroes and was taking them to a farm in the South. They were chained six and six together. A small iron clevis was around the left wrist of each, and this fastened to the main chain by a shorter one at a convenient distance from the others. The slaves were strung together like a string of fish. They, too, were being separated, as she had been, from the scenes of their childhood and families. These scenes all increased the despair she had experienced.

After some time, the steamboat creaked and groaned as it slowly inched its way up to the dock. Lewis and Minty had been told that they would be met and escorted to this strange new place they would be calling home. They anxiously scanned the crowd of onlookers for someone they may have already met, Jesse Grant. Exiting the boat by way of the gangplank, Minty felt as if she were still swaying from the motion of the boat. They had arrived at their destination, the small village of Point Pleasant which lay along the Ohio River, five miles southeast of New Richmond.

Lewis had made many trips to the Cincinnati area with General Clay. He told Minty that two things stood out that made New Richmond an attractive destination for freed and fugitive slaves—-its location on the Ohio River and the presence of an established black community. [According to the 1850 census, 412 black people are listed as residents in Clermont County, Ohio, and New Richmond was home to 256 of them. This included the O'Banions.]

Also, during the 19th century, New Richmond was home to a bustling riverboat industry and tobacco farms, attracting free black workers from states in the South. Many of these free blacks played an important role in helping slaves who fled Kentucky for New Richmond's shore. New Richmond became known as a "town of safety to anyone engaged in the pursuit of truth" regarding safety.

New Richmond was home to the Cranston Memorial Presbyterian Church, the church which was to become the forefront of the anti-slavery battle. The church later attracted abolitionist speakers such as Ripley's John Rankin, George Beecher, and Calvin Stowe, husband of Harriet Beecher Stowe.

The Jesse Grant home in Point Pleasant

The Anti-Slavery Society - one of the first in the country - met at the Cranston Memorial Presbyterian Church in January 1836. The church believed slavery was an abomination, and it favored freeing the slaves immediately. In July of 1836, the Cranston church passed a resolution to "withhold from communion all persons holding men, women or children as property or those who advocate the system.

Although Minty and Lewis had no schooling and were unable to read or write, they hoped that as freed blacks their children would receive an education here in Ohio. No schooling for blacks existed at the time of their arrival, but would soon gradually come into existence. Just outside New Richmond, the liberal Clermont Academy (or Parker Academy) was launched in 1839. It was one of the first schools in the country to offer a biracial, co-ed education. Clermont's students included the children of both former slaves and abolitionists. [The children of Minty and Lewis did receive an education, as indicated on census records.]

When Minty became a domestic for the newly married Jesse Grants, she was about thirty-two. Many people had been an influence in her life. First of all, the slave-holding Randolph family, secondly the slave holding Green Clay family, and now the Jesse Grant family, a family strictly against slavery. What a change for this little woman who had never known anything but slavery. Little did Minty realize that she was about to become "Nanny" to a baby boy destined to become President of the United States one day, none other than Ulysses S. Grant who was born in April of 1822. She would attend his infant life, rocking him as he rested against her broad bosom, and guiding his footsteps.

Chapter Eleven

Minty, Domestic of
Jesse Grant

Minty almost looked forward to her trips to the river's edge and her time of reminiscing. As she watched the driftwood washing ashore, her thoughts, which had no time frame, drifted back to when she arrived at Point Pleasant. She remembered how she had to become acquainted with a new home and a new employer, Jesse Grant. General Green Clay had fondly arranged for his loyal valet and Minty to find employment in this free state.

A whole new world had opened up to them. Who was this Jesse Grant (1794-1873) and how might the O'Banions have found employment with his family? Over the years spent with the Grants and others, Minty learned that this man had been described as a boisterous businessman, active in politics, bragging openly about his son, and, in fact, making Ulysses' life somewhat difficult at times. He was also described as an abolitionist and a buttinsky in his son's life, often creating much tension between father and son. He later even used his son's amazing success as a general to improve his leather shop business by using his name in an advertising jingle that he wrote:

Since Grant has whipped the Rebel Lee,
And opened trade from sea to sea,
Our goods in price soon advance;
Then don't neglect the present chance
To call on GRANT and PERKINS.

When still a youth, Jesse Grant's mother had died and his father was unable to support the large family. He moved with his two youngest children to Maysville, Kentucky, where his eldest son Peter lived; he more or less farmed the three middle children out, and left Jesse and a sister to fend for themselves. While Jesse scrambled to stay afloat, he learned the tannery trade. Jesse lived for a time with a Judge Tod who exhibited a stable influence on the young lad. He later lived in Ohio in the home of Owen Brown, father of John Brown, the anti-slavery martyr depicted in the song "John Brown's Body Lies a Moldering in the Grave".

This song originated with soldiers of the Massachusetts 12th Regiment and soon spread to become the most popular anthem of the Union soldiers during the Civil War. Many versions of the song exist, and one particularly well written version by William W. Patton follows:

MINTY, DOMESTIC OF JESSE GRANT

Old John Brown's body lies moldering in the grave,
While weep the sons of bondage whom he ventured all to save;
But tho he lost his life while struggling for the slave,
His soul is marching on.

John Brown was a hero, undaunted, true and brave,
And Kansas knows his valor when he fought her rights to save;
Now, tho the grass grows green above his grave,
His soul is marching on.

He captured Harper's Ferry, with his nineteen men so few,
and frightened "Old Virginny" till she trembled thru and thru;
They hung him for a traitor, themselves the traitor crew,
But his soul is marching on.

John Brown was John the Baptist of the Christ we are to see,
Christ who of the bondmen shall the Liberator be,
And soon thruout the Sunny South the slaves shall all be free,
For his soul is marching on.

The conflict that he heralded he looks from heaven to view,
On the army of the Union with its flag red, white and blue.
And heaven shall ring with anthems o'er the deed they mean to do,
For his soul is marching on.

Ye soldiers of Freedom, then strike, while strike ye may,
The death blow of oppression in a better time and way,
For the dawn of old John Brown has brightened into day,
And his soul is marching on.

[The Brown tune inspired Julia Ward Howe to write her lyrics for
the same melody, *The Battle Hymn of the Republic*.]

When Jesse left the Browns, he later apprenticed to his brother Peter as a tanner, and soon owned his own tannery in Ravenna, Ohio. In 1820, Jesse worked at a tannery in Bethel, Ohio for a short time until the owner of the tannery hired him as a foreman at his Point Pleasant, Ohio tannery. Jesse moved to Point Pleasant and rented a cabin next to the tannery.

In June of 1821, Jesse had married Hannah Simpson. This was about the time that Minty went to work as a domestic for them, and it wasn't long before she had a baby besides her own at her bosom. This baby was none other than Ulysses S. Grant.

Jesse had also opened a carriage service to western Ohio and points south. This carriage service would have been a profitable business for a young man. Stage coach lines in Kentucky had existed since the early 1800's.

John Brown's tombstone in North Elba, New York

The need for these early stages had begun in Lexington, Kentucky, the home of horse racing and the center for slave sales. Some of the lines ran from Lexington to the Olympian Springs, an ideal summer resort which could boast about their sulphur wells, the best music, dancing, bathing, hunting, riding, barbeques, and fish feasts, among other things. Who owned some of these resorts? None other than General Green Clay. Minty wondered if this carriage business was how the Green Clay family connected with Jesse Grant, providing a place for Lewis and Minty to begin their new life of freedom.

In 1823 Jesse bought forty acres from Thomas Morris in Georgetown, six miles to the northeast of

Tannery owned by Jesse Grant

the little town of Point Pleasant. He moved his family there and Minty went with them, continuing as a domestic and nanny to their children. In Georgetown, Jesse's industry, wealth, and family increased. He worked as a tanner, butcher, hauler, builder (he built the town jail), and he still owned a carriage- service and two small farms. Eventually he owned tanneries in Portsmouth, Kentucky on the Ohio River, a leather store in Galena, Illinois, and branch stores at La Crosse, Wisconsin and near Cedar Rapids, Iowa.

While with the Grants, Minty continued growing a family of her own. Five new babies were added to the O'Banion family. Minty remained with the Grants for about thirteen years, thereby caring for the other Grant offspring as well as her own and witnessing many of Ulysses' escapades.

Minty loved to share the tales of her young charge. She beamed with pride as she shared the fact that young Ulysses loved horses. Why, at age seven he began to gather wood for the house and tannery. Although he was still too small to carry the wood himself, others would stack it and later unload it. The young Grant drove the team himself. Four years later he was plowing the fields and took over all the work done with horses. [From his memoirs] Jesse Grant always ensured that his boys received an education, so Ulysses did his equestrian chores while attending school full-time. He soon developed a reputation within the family for his horsemanship. He is said to have been able to move about the horses with ease, while other boys his age would get kicked when attempting the same feats. Grant could control the animals and knew how to match a horse to a specific task, whether riding, pulling or plowing.

Minty may have looked something like this when working for the Grants

One horse story that Minty often shared, dogged the young Grant for the rest of his life, and continually stood to caution him that he was not a businessman. A neighbor of the Grants owned a beautiful colt that Ulysses

The home of Jesse Grant in Georgetown

wanted very badly. When the neighbor offered to sell the young horse for twenty-five dollars, Ulysses' father, Jesse Grant, countered by saying that the animal was worth but twenty. Nonetheless, the son, then only eight, persisted. His father finally relented, telling his son to first offer twenty; then, if refused, to offer twenty-two and a half; then, if refused again, to offer the full twenty-five. Grant rode quickly to the neighbor's and admitted later that he said, "Papa says I may offer you twenty dollars for the colt, but if you won't take that, I am to offer twenty-two and a half, and if you won't take that, I am to give you twenty-five." Not surprisingly, Grant purchased the colt for the full twenty-five. The village boys teased Grant as the story got out, and he forever regretted the transaction. One of the most hurtful aspects for him was that the embarrassment resulted from openness and honesty on his part, not trickery.

Minty highly favored Ulysses. For thirteen years she had watched him grow up and viewed many of his shenanigans while trying to avoid working in his father's tannery. Horses smelled much better.

Jesse and Hannah (Simpson) Grant

Tombstone of Jesse Grant

In 1833, shortly after she had given birth to a daughter named Henrietta, Minty left the Grants and moved with Lewis to Bethel where she found employment in various Clermont homes, while Lewis continued to work at odd jobs. Minty once again found herself getting used to new surroundings. She soon found herself surrounded by people highly involved in the abolitionist movement. Some of these included Senator Thomas Morris, publisher James Birney, and the Beecher family. [Note three counties related to Minty in Ohio.]

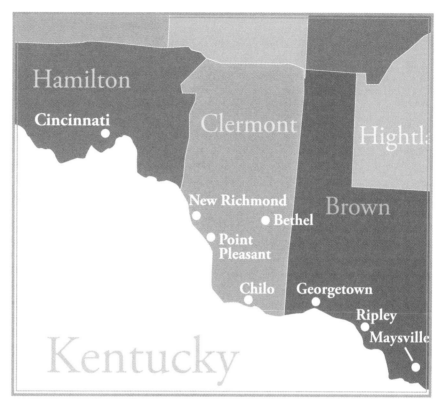

Map showing where the O'Banions lived in Ohio

Point Pleasant to New Richmond 4.7 miles
Point Pleasant to Georgetown 17 miles
Point Pleasant to Bethel 11.9 miles
Georgetown to Bethel 12.2 miles
New Richmond to Cincinnati 22 miles
Point Pleasant to Chilo 10.5 miles

Chapter Twelve

Minty and Senator Morris

(1776 – 1844)

inty had once again been saddened when leaving the Grants. She had been nursemaid to all of these children. They had been playmates with her little ones. They were like her own. But she soon had found herself busily engaged with new families and different atmospheres. She easily found employment after her family moved to Bethel, Ohio. Trustworthy domestics were in high demand, and with recommendations from Jesse Grant, who was also a highly political figure and an anti-slavery advocate, helped to relocate her.

Senator Thomas Morris (1776-1844), father of eleven children, became her employer. He had been found to be an interesting and kindly man. She learned that he had been taught to read by his mother from the Bible and books from his father's small library. Thomas Morris sort of represents the dream of many of the Americans on the new frontier. He was born a poor boy that wasn't well known, and through his intelligence and willingness to work hard he progressed through the political system to become a United States Senator from 1833 to 1839. He then became the first Senator to bring forth a challenge on slave holding. Many widely and cruelly criticized him for these efforts of introducing anti-slavery legislation to Congress. Minty listened intently and with compassion as he shared with his wife the taunts he faced regularly from his colleagues.

For instance, Henry Clay, the most popular senator of his time, accused the abolitionists of disrupting the harmony of the country. In response, Senator Morris stated that his hatred of slavery came from a favorite, Thomas Jefferson himself. Morris said, "In my infant years I learned to hate slavery. The Declaration of Independence, the words of Thomas Jefferson, and the free state in which he was born taught me it was wrong. I also, in early life, saw a slave kneel before his master, and hold up with as much apparent submission, humility, and adoration, as man would have done before his Maker, while his master, with outstretched rod, stood over him. This, I thought, is slavery—one man subjected to the will and power of another and the laws affording him no protection, and he has to beg pardon of man, because he has offended man, [not the laws] as if his master were a superior and all powerful being."

Morris couldn't understand how these political figures, Henry Clay included, and many of whom were slave holders themselves, talked about opposition to slavery while at the same time permitted the cursed traffic in slaves to be carried on in their midst, and if any of our citizens shall inform slaves they are free, they are indicted and found guilty of riot. As a result of his opposition, Morris was "read out" or expelled from his political position by the Democrats' refusal to re-elect him.

Truly, Thomas Morris was a friend of the slave and someone Minty was proud to work for. He gained much knowledge of the lives of the slaves from Minty. It grieved Minty to see the mistreatment of this kind man who tried to alleviate the pain of the slaves.

In a letter written to the editors of the Ohio Statesman, in defense of abolitionist Judge Tappan, Morris said, "When the hand and time shall point to the last hour of my existence, I trust that my fervent prayer may be that the Lord Almighty, in his own good time, will deliver the Negro race from the cruel slavery under which they are now groaning, and that the liberties and happiness of my country may be perpetual."

As a lawyer, Morris who did not consider himself as religious quoted the Bible in his arguments before the jury. At one time, he submitted a question to the Senate as to whom or what was the higher authority, the Senate or the Bible.

He taught his children to believe in Christ and to live by the Bible for Christian character. All of his children, except two, were firm in the faith and members of either the Methodist or Presbyterian Churches.

In a biography of Thomas Morris, written by his son B.F. Morris, B.F. states that his father felt that no one ought to live without exerting a good and active influence on his fellow-men. He exhibited this by being a friend to the poor and oppressed, and no honest person ever went away from his door without receiving sympathy and aid.

MINTY AND SENATOR MORRIS

A monument to Senator Thomas Morris reads, "A fearless advocate of human liberty." This newspaper article describes the erection of the monument in Thomas Morris' honor.

Thomas Morris lived by the following motto:

Faint not in all the weary strife. Though every day without toil be rife, Work is the element of life;— Action is light;—

For man was made to toil and strive, And only those who labor live.

Minty was especially fond of the kindly Mrs. Morris. Someone once said that behind every successful man there is a woman, and Rachel Morris, wife of Thomas Morris, was no exception. She had been reared in the midst of pioneer life, was a faithful participant in the great work of laying the foundations of this new empire. She was a fitting companion for this man, a woman who had been brought up with patient heroism to the dangers of a back-woods life. An example of her bravery shows through an incident involving her sister and herself. In 1796, Rachel and her sister made a visit to the family homestead in Washington, Mason County, Kentucky, and a distance of 45 miles. This was through unbroken wilderness, except by a horse path. Indians, roaming in the forests, were a constant danger. Even so, the girls started alone on horseback and safely accomplished their journey. They had only a linen wallet with some shelled corn in one end for their horses and their dinner in another. They stopped by a running stream, poured the corn on the ground for the horses, and ate their lunch on horseback. [During this time period, a son, Milford, was born to Minty (1837).]

MONUMENT TO THOMAS MORRIS.—A letter from one of the sons of Thomas Morris, of Ohio, to Mr. Gerrit Smith, informs that a large and beautiful monument has been erected to the memory of the incorruptible and fearless senator, who answered Henry Clay's great speech in defence of slavery, in 1839, and stood as the Liberty candidate for the Vice Presidency, along with the noble Birney, in 1844. It bears the following, fine inscription, as just as it is appropriate :

"THOMAS MORRIS,
late U. S. Senator,
was born January 3d, 1776.
Died December 7th, 1844.
Unawed by power, and uninfluenced by flattery, he was, through life,
the fearless advocate of
human liberty."

Emancipator.

Newspaper article describing monument given in honor of Thomas Morris

Minty and
James G. Birney

Others that Minty had worked for as a domestic often came to her mind. One of these was James G. Birney, a close friend of Senator Thomas Morris. Birney was the son of a James Birney wealthy Irish family who had settled in Kentucky. James grew up near Dansville, Kentucky and received a fine education. He attended college in Lexington, Kentucky and the College of New Jersey, becoming a lawyer.

He married in 1816 and began his political career that same year. He had received his first slave at the age of six, a gift from his father and more slaves as a wedding gift, and although he was a slave owner, owning forty-three in all which were worth a fortune, he joined with the minority group of legislators opposed to slavery.

He bought a cotton plantation in 1819 in Alabama and during this time took strong stances against slavery. He was unsuccessful in trying to get legislation passed which prohibited slaves being sold into Alabama from other states. His plantation was unsuccessful, mostly from his gambling habits, so he sold the plantation, sold his slaves to a friend, and returned to Kentucky and set up a law practice.

In 1834 he declared himself an abolitionist and freed his remaining slaves, and began the publication of his abolitionist paper in New Richmond. Minty was working for him at this time. She was a source of much information for his newspaper as to the slavery issue. He had tried to influence Kentuckians into emancipating slaves. This failed due to the opposition that Henry Clay and others had set forth in the years Birney was living out of state. He formed the Kentucky Anti-slavery Society, and went to New York to speak to the American Anti-slavery Society where he was associated with Thomas Morris, among others. He attempted to publish an anti-slavery newspaper, but no publisher would print it. Conflicts arose among conflicting interests. In spite of threats, he persisted and found a publisher in Cincinnati, although he still had to deal with opposition.

In 1836, James G. Birney launched *The Philanthropist* in Cincinnati. It was the first anti-slavery newspaper published in the west. The incendiary newspaper quickly drew scorn and violent threats from slave-owners in Birney's native Kentucky. Locals formed an armed vigilance committee to patrol the streets and protect the newspaper's office. It was Birney who had described New Richmond as a "town of safety to anyone engaged in the pursuit of truth" regarding slavery.

"The truth is Liberty and Slavery cannot both live long in juxtaposition," he wrote. "They are antagonist elements and know ... neither truce nor reconciliation. Either Liberty will stand on the lifeless body, rejoicing in the everlasting overthrow of her greatest enemy—or Slavery, with its chains and its scourges, its woes or its tears, will overspread our favored land."

An item in that newspaper announced that the "New Richmond Anti-Slavery Society will meet at the Presbyterian Church in New Richmond at early candle lighting on Saturday January 2 , 1836 , and that should the weather be pleasant , an address may be expected." This 1836 date is quite early for anti slavery activity, and New Richmond should be highly commended for having enough interest to sustain such meetings. These New Richmond people were not merely "anti slavery," most people were vaguely against slavery in principal, but these men were strong abolitionists who advocated, even demanded, that all slaves be immediately freed and the slavery system be ended. Records show that during the period 1836 until the Civil War ended New Richmond was a recognized center of abolitionist activity.

Despite the protection New Richmond offered, Birney grew tired of the 20-mile commute from his New Richmond home and decided to relocate the paper in Cincinnati in April of 1836. His publication, The Philanthropist, gained in circulation. During its first four months in Cincinnati, the Philanthropist's office was ransacked twice by anti- abolitionist mobs. These mobs caused by the pro-slavery element in Cincinnati had been existing for some time. They had been posting placards around the city warning the abolitionists to beware, and many threats of violence had been made against Birney. A public meeting had been held and a series of resolutions were adopted expressing abhorrence of the principles advocated by the abolitionists.

On January 22, 1836, an organized mob against his abolitionist paper gathered out front of his business. Birney sought help from the law but received no response. He himself confronted the mob about the evils of slavery and after persuading them, they dispersed.

On July 12 of that same year a mob of white Cincinnatians destroyed the newspaper's printing press. And on July 30, they "broke open the printing office of the *Philanthropist*, the abolition paper, scattered the type into the street, tore down the presses and completely dismantled the office. … A portion of the press was then dragged down the street and thrown into the river." [Cincinnati Gazette]

Burning Birney's printing press

Though the paper reopened in Cincinnati in September, Birney soon turned his attention to the political arena. He encouraged the development of a new party that became the Liberty Party and he was elected as the candidate in the presidential election of 1840 with Thomas Morris as his vice-president, but this was unsuccessful. [This year Minty had another daughter, Mary.]

Birney often lectured and the common theme of his lectures pointed to the unlawful methods of those favoring slavery. In 1837 he was elected as Secretary of the Anti- slavery Society, and after accepting it he moved with his family to New York. James G. Birney's claim to fame would probably be that he would become one of the nation's most famous and powerful abolitionists, a leader in the anti- slavery movement.

Chapter Fourteen

Church Involvement

All through this time of turmoil, Minty had found herself right in the midst of things. She had watched and listened as much history was being made. She knew firsthand many of the individuals involved. She cooked for them, cleaned for them, cared for them, and even wept for them.

CHURCH INVOLVEMENT

The Underground Railroad was becoming more alarmingly well-known, some states were banning education for blacks, and Anti-Slavery Societies were being formed. Many of the churches seemed to be at the forefront of the endeavor to arouse interest on behalf of the slave. One church in particular, the Cranston Memorial Presbyterian Church in New Richmond, took a lead in this. In terms of religious leadership, New Richmond's Cranston Memorial Presbyterian Church took the stand as to the anti-slavery battle in the Cincinnati area. The church hosted the organizational meeting of the New Richmond Anti-Slavery Society in 1836, shortly after Minty and Lewis left the employ of Jesse Grant. Anti-slavery speakers included James G. Birney, Calvin Stowe, George Beecher, and brothers John and Alexander T. Rankin.

This church took Lewis and Minty in as members, baptizing Lewis in 1839 and Minty in 1840. They were the first blacks taken in as members, and they became sextons of the church for the years 1841-1846 and received small payments. Minty received fifty cents for cleaning the Sunday School room. [Birney may well have been instrumental in Lewis and Minty's becoming members of the Cranston Presbyterian Memorial Church in New Richmond.]

Leading churches, throughout the North and the South, as far back as into the 1700's had preached the doctrine that slavery was a divinely ordained institution. This dogmatic doctrine split the churches, communities, families, and in many cases brought brother against brother. However, in 1780, Bishop Asbury was said to be the bitterest and most vigorous opponent of slavery in America of his time. He urged all churches, Methodists, Presbyterians, Baptists, and others, to take a stand against this terrible cancer, slavery. Pronouncements made at the Methodist Conference included: "any traveling preacher who holds slaves must give a promise to set them free", and "Slavery is contrary to the law of God, man, and nature, hurtful to society, contrary to … pure religion, and doing that which we would not want others to do to us." Still, the ruling minority stood firm in their belief that the white race was born to rule and the black race was born to serve.

Chapter Fifteen

Minty and the Beecher Family

Minty had become popular as a domestic among those involved with the abolitionist movement. She provided much information to the abolitionist movement. A third employer during this time period of Minty's life was the Lyman Beecher family. Lyman Beecher was the first president of the Lane Theological Seminary in Cincinnati and the father of Harriet Beecher Stowe, author of the famous antislavery novel, *Uncle Tom's Cabin*, which was credited with helping to fuel the abolitionist cause in the 1850's.

Lane Theological Seminary

The family was a prolific group of religious leaders, educators, writers, and antislavery and women's rights advocates. The Beecher family includes Harriet's sister, Catherine Beecher, an early female educator and writer who helped found numerous high schools and colleges for women; brother Rev. Henry Ward Beecher, a leader of the women's suffrage movement and considered by some to be the most eloquent minister of his time; General James Beecher, a Civil War general who commanded the first African-American troops in the Union Army recruited from the South; and sister Isabella Beecher Hooker, a women's rights advocate.

After their arrival in Cincinnati, the Beechers took up residence in a rented house until their permanent house was completed in Walnut Hills. It was a comfortable two-story brick house with a pretty garden, and a barn with a cow, horse and chickens. There were thirteen members of the family including two servants

The Beecher Family, Harriet is on the right

The Beecher house

who were to live in this residence. One of these was Minty for some time.

The Beechers lived in Cincinnati for nearly 20 years, from 1832 to the early 1850's, before returning to the East. Harriet had begun her novel in the early 1840's, and shortly after leaving Cincinnati in 1851-1852, Harriet Beecher Stowe published the best-selling book of its time, *Uncle Tom's Cabin*. It was a fictionalized popular account of the pain slavery imposed on its victims and of the difficult struggles of slaves to escape and travel on the

Underground Railroad to freedom in the northern states or Canada. Published just after the Fugitive Slave Laws were enacted by the U.S. Congress in 1850, the book made Harriet Beecher Stowe's name a household word in the United States.

Uncle Tom's Cabin has been published in over 75 languages and is still an important text used in schools all over the world. Written at a time when women did not vote, have legal rights, or even speak in public meetings, *Uncle Tom's Cabin* became an important part of the social fabric. It was thought to be one of the causes of the Civil War to break out and the southern slaves to be emancipated by President Abraham Lincoln, effective in 1863. *Uncle Tom's Cabin* is a remarkable example of how one person can make a huge impact to improve the lives of millions of people. Harriet humanized the black folk, whereas, most writers did not.

When Harriet Beecher Stowe produced Uncle Tom's Cabin, 300,000 copies were sold in America in one year. It was translated into a score of languages. She refused to take any credit for what she had written. She said, "I, the author of *Uncle Tom's Cabin*? No, indeed, I could not control the story; it wrote itself. The Lord wrote it, and I was but the humblest instrument in his hand. It all came to me in visions, one after another, and I put them down in words. To him alone be the praise."

When Harriet Beecher Stowe met President Abraham Lincoln in 1862, he is said to have exclaimed, "So you are the little woman who wrote the book that started this Great War!"

While at the Beechers, Minty became a favorite of Harriet. She remembered the hours she spent with Harriet, supplying her with valuable data for her novel, giving her ideas of the darkie idioms and superstitions. She shared stories of many of the hardships endured by the slaves, that she had witnessed or had heard about from Lewis and other slaves.

One of the characters in *Uncle Tom's Cabin*, Uncle Tom, was taken from the Shelby Plantation. Is it just a coincidence that there was an O'Banion slave holder in Shelby County, Kentucky? Possibly Lewis O'Banion had been one of this man's slaves before being sold to Green Clay. Harriet often used familiar names and events in her novel. It is said that a freed slave gave Harriet the suggestion for the character of Uncle Tom. That man was probably Lewis O'Banion, Minty's husband.

Minty was not the only one who had inspired Harriet. She knew of others who had also inspired Harriet by sharing their knowledge gained from runaway's slaves. One of these was John Rankin. Harriet pulled

Painting of Eliza, from Uncle Tom's Cabin

a real-life story from Rankin's Underground Railroad for her book. This character was Eliza Harris, a slave woman who crossed the Ohio River, near Ripley, on drifting ice with her child in her arms and sheltered in the home of Levi Coffin for several days.

Chapter Sixteen

Rankin and Parker

So many of the abolitionists involved with the Underground Railroad lived within a few miles of each other in this area on the Ohio River. Reverend John Rankin lived in Ripley, Ohio, a few miles west of Maysville, Ohio, which appears to be the main crossing point for the slaves following the North Star. One hundred steps led from Ripley to the house on the hill where the Rankins lived with their thirteen children.

Rankin claimed that he did not recognize the slaveholder's right to the flesh and blood and souls of men and women. He said: "My

The Rankin House

house has been the door of freedom to many human beings, but while there was a hazard of life and property, there was much happiness in giving safety to the trembling fugitives. They were all children of God by creation and some of them I believe were redeemed by the blood of the Lamb."

With its proximity to the river and its owner's fierce opposition to slavery, the Rankin home was a perfect choice to become a stopping point on the Underground Railroad. The following picture was taken from a window of the Rankin home. It shows the Ohio River with Kentucky on the opposite side and the one hundred steps leading up to it.

John Rankin credits his mother for having the most significant impact on his childhood. She "earnestly opposed the use of whiskey and tobacco, and zealously spoke against Free Masonry". She also strongly opposed

Photo taken from inside the home of Rankin, looking across the river to Kentucky

dance and frolicking in any form. Moreover, she led the family in prayer when his father was absent. Yet, the most important and lasting impression she instilled in John was her open, unyielding opposition to slavery. In this manner, her beliefs became the foundation for her children. The Rankin family was proud of never having lost a "passenger" on the Underground Railroad. Most of the 2,000 escaped slaves who traveled through Ripley stayed with the Rankins before being sent on to Levi Coffin, who was another source of information for *Uncle Tom's Cabin.*

John Parker, another Ripley abolitionist and former slave who was active in the Underground Railroad, wrote of Rankin, "At times attacked on all sides by masters seeking their slaves, (John Rankin and his sons) beat back their assailant, and held its threshold unsullied. A lighted candle stood as a beacon which could be seen from across the river, and like the North Star was the guide to the fleeing slave.

During the Antebellum years, Parker became an important, if unheralded, conductor on the Underground Railroad, risking his life to aid more than nine hundred fugitive slaves in their journey to freedom. Parker also recruited soldiers for the Twenty-seventh United States Colored Troops during the Civil War.

Parker was born into slavery in Virginia, taught himself to read, later attended college, worked as a stevedore, saved his money and bought his freedom, and created a successful foundry. He also supplied Harriet Beecher Stowe with information for her book.

At night, Rankin ran a lantern to the top of a flagpole as a beacon to runaway slaves looking for a place of safety after crossing the Ohio River. Whenever Parker brought a slave from Kentucky to the Ohio River, he looked for that light signal before crossing.

Home of John Parker, Ripley abolitionist

Chapter Seventeen

The Underground
Railroad,
Levi Coffin

Whenever a funeral procession was seen wending its way toward the little cemetery southeast of town, Minty's mind would wander back to the time of the death of her husband Lewis and events surrounding it. During this time in Minty's life, the 1830's and up until the start of the Civil War, the Underground Railroad was becoming more and more public. All during this time, Minty worked as a domestic in the homes of those who were some-how a part of the abolitionist movement. She gained a first-hand awareness of what was happening behind the scenes, especially from

Mrs. Stowe who had become friends with Levi Coffin, the president of the Underground Railroad. This man had been involved with the movement since he was fifteen when at a corn husking he helped a kidnapped free black escape from a slave trader. Over the next several years Minty would learn much about the movement and just who Levi Coffin was.

Painting of escaping slaves

For one thing, she learned that the term Underground Railroad came into use at this time. It was a railroad with no rails and no whistles, a railroad of whispers and passwords. It was a railroad of silent figures following worn fences, traveling low in swamp lands and high thickets. Wild animals, snakes, lakes, rivers, and insects brought fear. However, these people were more fearful of looking back than meeting the unknown dangers lying ahead. They moved through a network of tunnels, farms, haystacks, houses, and other stranger places. Hiding in barns, cellars, attics, and forests, passengers moved secretly northward. They moved by foot, by wagon, by rail.

Levi Coffin and Catherine Coffin

They moved with an ear to the South and hope toward the North. They just kept moving. This was the Underground Railroad.

The name "Underground Railroad" may simply have evolved because its operators adopted the railroad vocabulary to camouflage their activities. Fugitive slaves from the South, looking for freedom in the North, were called "passengers". The hiding places were "stations". Groups of passengers traveled along "lines", "agents" ran stations, and "conductors" guided passengers between stations. Stations were located ten to fifteen miles apart so that a conductor could reach his dropping point and return home the same night. For the sake of secrecy and safety, few names were known. Instead, passwords were used. Upon arrival at a station, the conductor would ask, "Could you give food and shelter to one or more persons?" A "yes" reply would mean that the passengers would be received.

Sympathy for fugitive slaves grew in the North as tales of atrocities were heard. The auction block which divided families with no compassion from their owners, whippings, and other tortures aroused peoples' passion and concern for these humans who were treated as property. The Underground Railroad system probably began in Pennsylvania with the Quakers. The belief that all life was sacred moved them to help the persecuted.

Over time, regular routes were established along with sympathizers who were willing to risk their lives to help. Because secrecy was so necessary, many of the details of these operators remained unknown. What is known is that men and women who allowed the system to work were moral and courageous people. No written records were kept.

For the Underground Railroad to operate, workers were necessary. Over time many of those involved have become known. The person who has been considered the president of the Underground Railroad was Levi Coffin (1798-1877). His home became known as the Grand Central Station of the Railroad.

Levi was a member of the Committee on Concerns of People of Color to Consider Their Education and was treasurer of funds to aid the poor

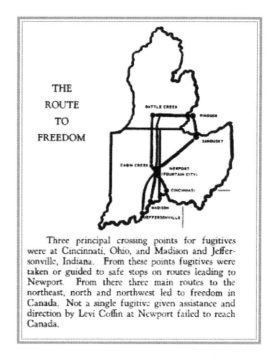

THE ROUTE TO FREEDOM

Three principal crossing points for fugitives were at Cincinnati, Ohio, and Madison and Jeffersonville, Indiana. From these points fugitives were taken or guided to safe stops on routes leading to Newport. From there three main routes to the northeast, north and northwest led to freedom in Canada. Not a single fugitive given assistance and direction by Levi Coffin at Newport failed to reach Canada.

Map showing routes taken by escaping slaves

William Bush gravestone

The Coffin House

and destitute. He was also active in the Temperance movement.

Levi and Catherine Coffin never knew when passengers would arrive, but there was rarely a week when none did. Frequently, several wagonloads from different lines of the Railroad arrived on the same night, by accident. Then the floor would be covered with men and women getting a little rest before moving on to the next station. So successful was the Coffin sanctuary that, while in Newport, Indiana, not a single slave failed to reach freedom.

From Indiana the Railroad made its way to Michigan. Michigan's neighbor to the north was Canada. That country had abolished slavery in 1792. Michigan's Constitution also prohibited slavery (1835). This made the state of Michigan a natural conduit to freedom. The Adrian line was the Quaker route. This route came from near Cincinnati, where Harriet Beecher Stowe operated a station. Cassopolis, Michigan was the meeting place of three lines from Indiana. Coldwater was the beginning point for a line leading directly northwest to Union City and then on to Marshall or Battle Creek, where Erastus Hussey was in charge. Battle Creek was a major switching point where routes from Ohio and Indiana met. They were combined and led to Marshall and then on to Detroit where fugitives were ferried across to Canada. Here the fugitives became free citizens and subjects of the British monarchy. It is estimated that the Underground Railroad in Michigan delivered between 40,000 and 50,000 runaways to freedom in Canada.

Coffin estimated that on the average he helped over one hundred runaways

Slaves would be transported in this false bottomed wagon

escape annually. Coffin's home became the convergence point of three major escape routes from Madison, New Albany, and Cincinnati. The runaways gathered at his home and at times two wagons were required to transport the escapees further north. Coffin would move them from his home to the next stop during the night. His home saw thousands of fugitives pass through, and it became known as the "Grand Central Station of the Underground Railroad."

Slaves were hidden in this attic.

Painting showing the Coffins taking in runaways—Charles Webber

[The Coffin House in Newport, Indiana was purchased in 1967 by the State of Indiana. The house was restored and then opened to the public in 1970. The site is a registered National Historic landmark and is operated by the Levi Coffin House Association.

In 1847, the Coffins moved to Cincinnati so that Levi could operate a wholesale warehouse which supplied goods to free labor stores. The Coffins continued to assist the cause, helping another 1,300 slaves escape.

Business with the Underground Railroad continued on briskly up to the outbreak of the Civil War and a year afterward, that is, before slaves were received and protected inside the

Union military lines. The friends of fugitives had increased in number and Levi Coffin had less difficulty in raising means for the passage, or in finding safe shelter. Mr. Coffin often raised money, bought tickets, and forwarded the fugitives by rail to Detroit, Sandusky, and other points on the lakes, when it was not likely hunters were ahead of them. After President Lincoln issued the Emancipation Procla-

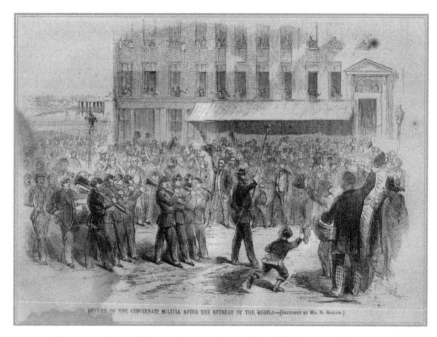

The return of the militia, gathering in front of the Coffin House in Cincinnati

mation in January of 1863, the Underground Railroad with its depots and conductors went out of business.

But, did this stop its president? No, he stepped down from this position and filled another desperately needed position, one involving the freed slaves (Freedmen). The Coffins had moved to Cincinnati, where he owned a store in which he refused to carry any goods that had been made by slaves. He became heavily involved in Free-labor organizations and traveled widely throughout the south and north promoting the selling and/or buying of only free labor goods.

When the Coffins moved to Cincinnati, and as an abolitionist, he became friends with the Beecher family and provided Harriet with many stories of runaway slaves, many of which she used in her novel.

When the war started, the Coffins were living in Cincinnati and in the thick of things. He had a front row seat to what was happening in the area. [Reminiscences of Levi Coffin, the Reputed President of the Underground Railroad.]

He related that when the war began prayer meetings were established in the churches and among the businessmen. Prayers were made that peace would be restored and brotherly love would come to our land, but the attendees could make no mention of ending slavery. This was so no feelings of some good brother would be hurt.

When the war began and Cincinnati was fearful of attack from the rebels, companies were formed with orders for every male regardless of age, color, or country to report to the voting places to be organized. Many women and children were sent out of the city for safety. Companies of volunteers arrived hourly from all over the state, whether judges, lawyers, preachers, professors, students, as well as farmers armed with their squirrel guns, referred to as "Squirrel Hunters". Arms and ammunition and soldiers from all over the state were ordered. Over 100,000 men were soon in Cincinnati. Women had tables spread all over the city fully supplied with provisions. Public halls and other places were used for lodging, and Coffin's own basement kitchen was used as a depository for victuals between meals. The large kitchen stove kept tea and coffee readily available.

The military confronted Levi himself for refusing to be compelled to report for duty because it was against his belief in Jesus' teaching to love your enemies; however, he did consider it right to care for the sick and feed the hungry. They bothered him no further. Mrs. Coffin gave blankets to some who had none. The Coffin house seemed to be more of a military post than an underground depot.

The Negro element was utterly ignorant of drilling, and some neglected to report because they were not regarded as citizens, while others hid. They were then discovered and dragged in.

In the fall of 1862 two large armies were gathered in Kentucky and Tennessee and many bloody battles were fought. Many slaveholders fled south, taking their able- bodied slaves with them and leaving the women and children and the sick to take care of themselves. They had no provisions because the armies consumed anything available.

Homeless, and with few possessions, blacks began fleeing to Union lines for protection. They found themselves as dependent on the Federal government for their existence as they had been on their masters.

Thousands gathered within Union army lines and were sent by boat up river. Some were brought to Cincinnati and dropped off at the docks with no provisions and no place to go. Coffin was called upon to help. The colored people already living in Cincinnati acted nobly, taking as many as they could take care of. The O'Banions were surely among those. Several thousands were sent on to Cairo, Illinois where they were housed in old military barracks. Upon hearing of the great destitution and suffering there, Levi went to investigate. He found no bedding, no cooking utensils, scanty rations issued by the government, few necessities, and many suffering with colds and coughs and an outbreak of smallpox. A young couple looking to start a school for blacks in the south started one at these barracks.

After the Emancipation Proclamation on January 1, 1863, Levi Coffin had begun to work for the Freedmen (freed slaves), collecting bedding, clothing, and money. His investigation led to The Western Freedmen's Aid Commission being organized in January of 1863, comprised of members from different religious denominations with Coffin acting as

Arrival of contrabands to Union camps

general agent. General Grant gave free transportation for all supplies for the freedmen and agents and teachers.

Coffin traveled extensively throughout the South raising money and collecting needed items, as well as visiting the sick and wounded in hospitals, some of which were just old plantation mansions.

Coffin tells one story involving the conditions of the freed slaves. He witnessed the arrival of a company of contrabands as they were called. They were brought in by a company of cavalry scouts, and rode, part in a wagon to which four mules were attached, part in an elegant carriage, drawn by a span of bay horses. The cavalry had been out in pursuit of a band of guerillas, and had gathered up these Negroes from the plantation of a rich planter, whose house had been the headquarters of the guerillas. The contrabands were quite jubilant at the prospect of liberty, and collected in a semicircle around the superintendent's tent to have their names and ages registered. Levi tells of this group:

One old woman, whose hair was white as wool, stood and after first, she was asked her age, he then proceeded to put the same question to others.

She replied:"Don't know, Massa, dey tole me I was twenty-one and made me do de work of a gal. I s'pose I's seventy-five or eighty."

The chaplain put her down as seventy-five. They could not tell how old they were, and he had to register their names and guess at their ages... When this was done the old woman made a speech to us, part of it amusing and part quite pathetic.

She said: "Yesterday when de sojers come I wal out milkin' de cows and prayin dat de Lord would send de Yankees here. Massa had tried to scare us; he told us if the Yankees got hold of us dey would work us mos' to death, then send us off to Cuba and sell us, but de Lord didn't tell me so, and I kep' prayin' dat dey would come. While I was milkin' I happened to raise my head, and bless de Lord, dere was de Yankees' heads poppin' up above de fence. Oh, my heart almos' jumped out of me for joy. Dey come right up and surrounded de house; de rebs was gone but massa was dere.

I quit milkin' and walked right by de captain. He said for us all to get ready, he was going to take us out of slavery. Oh, dat made me feel good. I took de bucket of milk into de kitchen and set it down, and went out into de yard and tole de captain how dey had used us and how dey bad 'bused us, all right before massa's face and he dasn't cheep. De boys was plowin' in de field and de captain sent sojers to tell 'em to unhitch de mules and hitch 'em to de wagon and I tell you dey did it mighty quick. Dey put four mules to de wagon, den dey fetched out de fine carriage and fine horses and made em' ready. Den we fetched out our old bags and old beds and put in de wagon. and de captain tole us to put in provisions to eat. I tell you it was all done mighty quick, and we drove OK some of us ridin' in de fine carriage and de rest in de wagon.—De sojers went before and behind us, and here we all is, bless de Lord. I ...

All listened with intense interest to the old woman's story, told in her own simple language.

She pointed to several of the company, and said, "Dese are my children and grandchildren," then turning to us, she continued, "Gent'men, dis is all de work of de Lord. I has been prayin' many years dat he would send deliverance to us poor slaves, and my faith never failed me dat he would hear my prayer, and dat I would live to be free."

She then broke into a song of praise and thanksgiving, in which others joined her, singing in that peculiar, plaintive manner characteristic of the musical utterances of slaves— those who sing from the depths of heart experience.

Levi Coffin said that he was renewedly convinced that many of the Lord's children were to be found among the poor untutored slaves.

Later, Mr. Coffin spent three years in England raising funds to help the Freedmen.

Many tears were shed by Minty and those close to her over these years as war clouds drifted nearer and nearer. Thoughts of her loved ones crowded her mind whenever she heard of some escapee or the situations under which they were forced to live. It was known that some of the Green Clay slaves were with the Union army and some were with the Confederate army. Could some of these be hers?

Chapter Eighteen

Dismal *Swamp*

All during this time while Minty was working for these families involved in the Underground Railroad she heard tale after tale of runaway slaves who didn't go to the North. It was not until after 1830 that the northern states began to aid the runaways. The Fugitive Slave Act meant that the runaways would probably be recaptured and sent back to their owners. Therefore, many individuals who fled the plantations headed toward swampy areas rather than heading north. They knew that it would be difficult for slave catchers and bloodhounds to follow them. Runaways, especially

Painting showing the horror faced by escaping slaves in the Great Dismal Swamp

from the eastern states of Virginia and the North Carolina, entered the area known as the Great Dismal Swamp. [See picture above] Minty also learned much about this area known as the Dismal Swamp from Harriet Beecher Stowe who was in the process of gathering information for a follow-up novel to *Uncle Tom's Cabin* which was entitled *Dred*. The title character is an escaped slave and religious zealot who aids fellow slaves and spends most of his time plotting a slave rebellion.

Bears seen in the Dismal Swamp

This swamp was a morass of huge trees towering over dense underbrush and delicate ferns, inhabited by black bears, wildcats, wild cattle and hogs, and poisonous snakes. It provided a natural refuge for runaways.

The slaves established colonies on high ground where they built crude huts. Family life evolved and the abundant animal life provided food and clothing. These slaves became known as maroons.

The Great Dismal Swamp that runs through Virginia and North Carolina is about 200 square miles of mud, bugs, bears, snakes, thorns, and quicksand. It stretches from thirty-seven miles

Sketch of a slave attacking a snake

long to twelve miles wide. The maroons farmed the higher, drier areas. It is unknown as to the exact number of slaves that escaped their oppressors and found refuge in the Dismal Swamp, but it is estimated that the number is over one thousand.

This swampy ground actually reaches down into Georgia and Florida and estimates claim it covers over a thousand square miles.

Painting by David Edward Cronin of Dismal Swamp

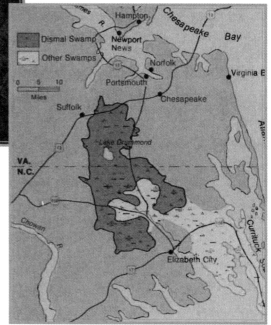

Map showing Dismal Swamp

Chapter Nineteen

Antebellum Years

Minty often reminisced about their life as a family in those years before the Civil War. They were freed slaves living in the world of the whites in the area of Cincinnati, a southern city in a northern state. Only a river separated them from slavery. Minty found herself and her family accepted by the abolitionists, but not well by the rest of the whites. Much racism existed in Ohio. Numerous laws had been enacted denying blacks their rights. The laws prohibited black men from voting, serving on juries, testifying in court against whites, renting or leasing land, receiving assistance at the "poor house", or sending their children to public school. If a black were found to be idle, he could be punished by being sent to a chain gang to work.

As far back as 1829, violence against free blacks had been rampant in the Cincinnati area. In fact, more than half of Cincinnati's African American residents had been driven out of the city by white mob violence. These riots ushered in more than a century-long period of violence against Northern blacks. Perhaps the relationships Minty had with the abolitionists prevented violence against them.

Before 1860 the O'Banion family had grown to eighteen, not counting grandchildren, although many of them were still slaves in Kentucky, belonging to descendants of Green Clay. Some of them may even have been sold. General Green Clay's will of 1834 lists the first names of over one hundred of his slaves and indicates to which of his children each will go. Ten slaves were emancipated.

Undoubtedly, some of these were descendants of Minty and Lewis. Employment was no easy task for the freed blacks. They were limited to discriminatory jobs; whereas, in the South they had been forced to perform all types of labor, thus becoming skilled workers. The whites did not want blacks infringing on the skilled worker jobs. Since rampant discrimination made it unlikely that a family could be supported on one salary, Lewis worked at whatever odd jobs he could find, and Minty found work as a domestic in various homes. The children had to take care of each other. Those old enough to work outside the home helped support the family. Their home was on the outskirts of the city where the rest of the blacks lived.

The domestic work open to black women was often steady, unlike many seasonal jobs available to men. One attractive feature of domestic work in the homes of others, or of "taking in" washing or sewing at one's own home, was that such an arrangement allowed for the care of children at the workplace.

As for the children of freed slaves obtaining an education, they were denied public education or were segregated in underfunded substandard schools in most northern schools. A few African-Americans managed to achieve some academic education in classes conducted secretly under the guise of trade schools for learning such skills as sewing, cooking, and carpentry. As sections of the South fell to the Union more schools opened for blacks. Education in Ohio remained unorganized and unregulated until the 1840s. A new state system came into being in 1849, modeled on the Akron School Law of 1847, which established school boards, tax systems to pay for public school systems, school districts based on geography, and a graded system of advancement. Blacks and mulattoes were not taxed because their children were not legally allowed to attend the new public schools in Ohio. For the most part, black children were so few that white community members did not feel they posed a threat and these children were permitted to attend public schools. Meanwhile, blacks in Cincinnati and Columbus managed to collect funds to operate their own schools.

In 1853 the state modified the law to require boards of education to provide schools for black children in districts where more than twenty lived; however, the schools were grossly unequal in quality. (Census records indicate that the O'Banion children had been allowed schooling because they were listed as being able to read and write.)

Were Minty and Lewis ever able to know what was happening in the lives of their "left behind" children? It is not known, but one can imagine that they were. In antebellum Cincinnati, the blacks knew that the Dumas Hotel was a place to gather information on people and conditions in the South. Visiting slaveholders often lodged their personal servants at the Dumas. While the owners pursued their business in the city, their slaves sought the company of Cincinnati blacks. Information was regularly exchanged, and many migrants maintained contact with loved ones through this link. Letters could even be smuggled. During the antebellum decades, the Dumas became a kind of underground post office. The underground communication network was the answer. Black seamen and boatmen were vital message carriers. The water routes offered an important source of income for blacks.

Not only could Minty have learned about her Kentucky family from the underground post office, but another source was Cassius Marcellus Clay who had his newspaper in Cincinnati.

One main characteristic of free black households was the number of boarders, individuals coming especially from the same area as had the host. This provided extra income for households. Some of these boarders were actually runaway slaves. Because of their close involvement with abolitionists, Minty and Lewis could very well have been a part of the Underground Railroad.

During the 19th century, the town was home to a bustling riverboat industry and tobacco farms, attracting free black workers from states like Mississippi. Just outside New Richmond, the liberal Clermont Academy (or Parker Academy) was launched in 1839. It was one of the first schools in the country to offer a biracial, co-ed education. Clermont's students included the children of both former slaves and abolitionists. Ohio's first constitution described education as "essentially necessary to good government." Cincinnati's first superintendent of education urged public education to "Americanize" immigrant children so that they might embrace principles of republicanism. One of the purposes of the common schools was that of as eliminating the problem of "youth who roam the streets of our cities and towns, growing up ignorant in all that is good, and wise in all that is evil."

Chapter Twenty

Abraham Lincoln

Train whistles whistling mournfully in the night hours often brought to Minty's mind Abraham Lincoln. He was probably the most famous president to cross the stage of Minty's life, the man who ushered in the freedom for slaves. He is regarded as one of the greatest presidents of all time; however, in his first election in 1860, he was defiled, ridiculed and threatened, and won with a minority of the popular vote.

In spite of his becoming a great president, many looked upon Lincoln as a great failure. Many, as well, would look at his life and consider him a loser. Lincoln was born in Hardin County, Kentucky, about 100 miles west of where Minty lived as a slave of Green Clay in 1808. At age seven he and his parents were forced out of their home. Then his mother died when he was nine. As a result, he never finished grade school, let alone high school or college. But this did not prevent his continued learning. At twenty- three he tried to start a business, but it failed. He then tried politics, running for an office in his state and lost. Then he lost his job. He wanted to go to law school but couldn't get in. At twenty-four he borrowed money to start another business, but it failed, too, and he spent the next seventeen years trying to pay off the debt.

At twenty-six he got engaged, but his fiancée died before the wedding. At twenty-seven he had a total nervous breakdown and spent six months in bed. You would have expected him to quit. At twenty-nine he tried politics again, running for his state legislature; he lost again. Two years later he tried again and lost. Three years later he ran for Congress again and actually won, but two years later when he ran for reelection, he was, of course, defeated. Giving up on national politics for the time being, he sought a more humble job as a land officer in his home state, but he was rejected. He then had the bad judgment to run for the U.S. Senate twice (he lost both times) and then sought to be his party's nominee for vice president and failed again. It seemed as though he was a loser, but he wasn't a quitter. When he was fifty-one, after a lifetime of failure and loss, Abraham Lincoln ran for president and won. He ended slavery, led the country through the Civil War, and preserved the union of the United States. He did not give up. Each time he picked himself up, dusted himself off, and tried again. After several years of hardship, first in Kentucky, then in Indiana and Illinois, Lincoln set out on his own at the age of twenty-two, working as a wood splitter, shopkeeper, postmaster, and store owner.

He joined the militia when the Black Hawk War broke out, but the only action he saw was swatting mosquitoes. Then he went into politics. His early view of slavery was that it was not so much a moral issue, but as an impediment to economic development.

While Minty was busy in Ohio working as a domestic in the homes of various abolitionists, Lincoln was becoming established politically, getting married, and beginning a family. During this time, Lincoln's view toward slavery moved more toward moral indignation. Though Lincoln felt that blacks were not equal to whites, he did believe that America's founders intended that all men were created with certain inalienable rights. From here, though unpopular, he went on to become president.

Lincoln himself said that he was not a member of any Christian Church, but that he did believe in the Scriptures. He was much interested in psychic phenomena and paid close attention to his dreams, taking them seriously. In fact, he had a dream about his death.

The Lincolns did not escape the gripping sadness which spread countrywide. Mrs. Lincoln lost three of her Confederate brothers to the war.

In spite of his being labeled as a loser, Lincoln was looked up to by the blacks as an inspiration. When he was down, he never stayed down. Rather he picked himself up dusted himself off, and reentered the fight. If he could do it, so could they. What with the starvation and poor housing they were faced with, his example showed that they, too, could overcome.

In his painting of the boyhood of Lincoln, Eastman Johnson shows forth the quality of character of Lincoln that is not that of a loser, but rather that of determination to get ahead. The boy Lincoln did his reading at night by the light of the fireplace. He himself said that the only schooling he had was attending A B C schools by littles, littles that did not even amount to one year.

ABRAHAM LINCOLN

*The Boyhood of Lincoln, by Eastman Johnson Painting in
the Branch County Library in Coldwater, MI*

Chapter Twenty-One

The Civil War

With the onslaught of the Civil War, a war that had been brewing for several years, Minty, now in her seventies, was driven to tears again and again. First of all, she lost Lewis, her husband of almost sixty years and the father of their eighteen children. Then to add to her grief she watched as three of her grandsons marched off to war for the Union side, one of them being killed in the battle of Petersburg in Virginia. Some of the slave owners at the beginning of the war sold their slaves to the South. This brought further anxiety to Minty concerning her "left-behind" family in

Kentucky. Were some of them sold? Would she ever see them again? At least while they were still in Kentucky she knew where they were. Also, might not some of them be fighting on the Confederate side?

Minty continued working as a domestic in various homes in and around Cincinnati. Although she had never learned to read nor write, she was forever learning. She had never forgotten the years she spent with the Clay and Grant families. Their children were her "chilluns" and she never tired of hearing news about them. Her

General Ulysses Grant of the Union Army

special ones were Ulysses Grant, now a general in the Union Army and Cassius Marcellus Clay, abolitionist and newspaper owner. With the war coming closer, she hungered for news of Ulysses. She had followed his career, his appointment to West Point, his assignment with the Fourth U.S. Infantry, his marriage to Julia Dent, his financial difficulties, working for his father, and rejoining the military.

Minty's grandsons were anxious to enlist. Her tales of Grant's escapades as a youngster had instilled a desire in her grandsons of wanting to serve with him. But they would have to wait. When the war started, black men had rushed to enlist but were rejected because of a law that barred

Negroes from bearing arms. This law was later abolished and blacks were allowed to serve in artillery and infantry and performed all noncombatant support functions that sustain an army.

Black carpenters, chaplains, cooks, guards, laborers, nurses, scouts, spies, steamboat pilots, surgeons, and teamsters served as well.

When the grandsons were finally allowed to enlist, a sad grandmother bade them farewell, asking them to write even though she couldn't read.

Someone would read their letters to her. She wanted to know all about their army life, how they were treated, if they were well, if they had enough to eat. She wanted any news about General Grant. She was so proud of him. He was one of her boys, too. She hoped her grandsons would get to see him. She had made him their hero over the years.

Even though blacks were not allowed to be in the military, in 1862, when Cincinnati feared impeding danger from Morgan's Raiders, blacks were conscripted to fortify the city. Cruel conscripting squads, for four days of barbarous and inhumane treatment, dragged the greater part of the male population from home and across the river. For three weeks this Black Brigade labored on the fortification and then returned home.

Approximately 180,000 blacks, both free and escaped slaves, comprised 163 units which served in the Union Army and many more served in the Union Navy. They made up about ten percent of the entire Union Army, with about twenty percent, over 316,000 of all enrollees losing their lives.

The U.S. Colored Troops in the Civil War faced many different forms of racism. They were paid less than the white soldiers and assigned manual labor such as digging trenches. They were commended by their officers for their good conduct during a period of severe marching, and reductions of rations, amounting to almost absolute destitution. Not often engaged in battle, they were involved in a major battle of The Crater at Petersburg.

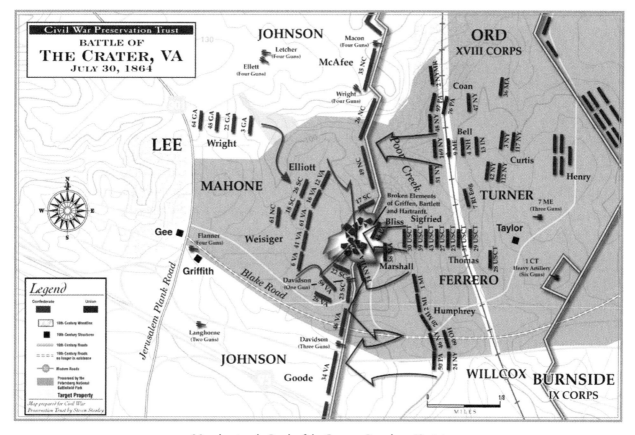

Map showing the Battle of the Crater at Petersburg, Virginia

General Grant intended to capture the vital city of Petersburg, located south of Richmond. Petersburg was a strategic crossroads and railroad hub which supplied Richmond and Lee's army with supplies. Its loss would make Richmond indefensible.

The two armies faced each other about 400 feet apart. The Confederate defenses continually stopped the Union atttacks. One of General Burnside's divisions, the 48th Pennsylvania Volunteer Infantry was made up mostly of coal miners who devised a plan for breaking through the

Confederate lines. Their plan was to dig a mine tunnel running from their lines to underneath the Confederate defenses, then to pack it with explosives. When the Confederte defenses were blown up, the Union Army could take the Confederates by surprise and rush in and take the city. The plan was approved by Grant and Burnside.

The black troops had been selected by their general, Burnside, to lead the assault, but plans were changed at the last minute by General Meade, and they were to be the last to go in. A slaughter! Their terrible losses tell how well they stood their ground.

The plan had been that Ferrero's division of United States Colored Troops (about 4,300 strong) would lead the assault, having been drilled in the use of ladders and instructed to move along the sides of the crater to secure the breach in the Confederate lines while the Confederates were still confused. Then with Ferrero's men holding the gap, Burnside's other divisions would cross the opening and take the city. However, the plan was changed by General Meade who claimed that if the assault failed, they would be accused of trying to get rid of the Negro troops. Therefore, three white divisions would make the initial charge with the colored troops following. These white troops had not had any training.

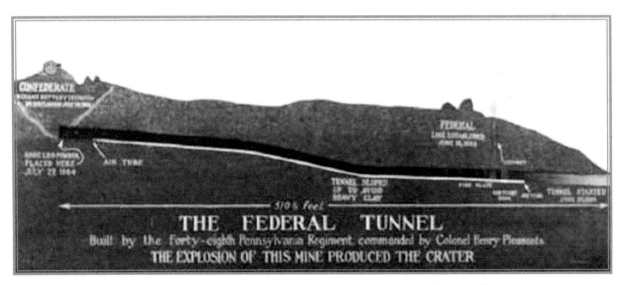

The tunnel dug by the Union soldiers at Petersburg where Minty's grandson was killed

When the blast came, it made a crater at least 170 feet long, 60 to 80 feet wide, and 30 feet deep. At least 278 Confederates were killed. The advancing force went down into the crater instead of as the plan had called for and became sitting ducks for the Confederates who soon rallied and stopped the attack. About 15,000 troops filled and surrounded the crater. The deadly battle cost the Union around 3,793 killed, wounded, or captured. The Confederates lost around 1,500.

A sad, sad day for Minty who soon learned that her grandson was one of the fallen. One consolation for her was the fact that her grandson had seen the hero of his grandmother's many stories, General Ulysses S. Grant.

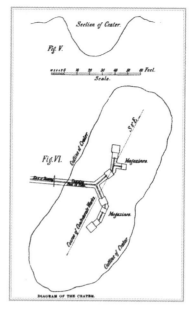

A diagram of the Crater at Petersburg

Regiment	Killed	Wounded	Missing	Total
23rd U.S. Colored Infantry	74	115	121	**310**
29th U.S. Colored Infantry	21	56	47	**124**
31st U.S. Colored Infantry	27	42	66	**135**
43rd U.S. Colored Infantry	14	86	23	**123**
30th U.S. Colored Infantry	18	104	78	**200**
39th U.S. Colored Infantry	13	97	47	**157**

Casualties In Ferrero's Division At The Battle Of The Mine
July 30, 1864.

Regiment	Killed	Wounded	Missing	Total
28th U.S. Colored Infantry	11	64	13	**88**
27th U.S. Colored Infantry	9	46	90	**75**
19th U.S. Colored Infantry	22	87	6	**115**
Totals	**209**	**697**	**421**	**1,327**

Nearly 40,000 black soldiers died over the course of the war—30,000 of infection or disease. Black soldiers served in artillery and infantry and performed all noncombat support functions that sustain an army, as well. Black carpenters, chaplains, cooks, guards, laborers, nurses, scouts, spies, steamboat pilots, surgeons, and teamsters also contributed to the war cause. There were nearly 80 black commissioned officers. Black women, who could not formally join the Army, nonetheless served as nurses, spies, and scouts.

By war's end, black soldiers made up roughly ten percent of the Union army. Approximately 179,000 black soldiers wore the blue.

A lone soldier sits in the midst of the crater.

Chapter Twenty-Two

Civil War *Camp Life*

M inty always looked forward to mail from her grandsons. She was anxious to know how they were faring and what their camp life was like. She knew where these three were, but she also thought about her other family in the Confederate army. What she learned was that camp life for the most part could be described as boring, mischievous, fearful, disease ridden, and life threatening.

Black soldiers learned forcefully the continued inequities of American life. They were separated into black regiments, with their camps separate from the whites, paid at a lower rate than white soldiers, denied the opportunity to become commissioned officers, often ill-used by commanders whose mode of discipline resembled that of slave masters, and frequently assigned to menial duties rather than combat, His tent was his home and the army camp was his community.

Several things often made camp life miserable. For one, wet weather produced mud, mud, and more mud, and dry weather brought dust, dust, and more dust.

A typical scene of meal preparations for Civil War soldiers

About three quarters of a soldier's time was spent in the army camp. Boredom stalked the armies almost as often as did hunger. When not faced with the terrors of battle, the days in camp tended to drag endlessly. A typical day began at 5 A.M. in the summer and 6 A.M. in the winter, when he was awakened by reveille.

After the first sergeant took the roll call, the men ate breakfast, and then prepared for their first of as many as five drill sessions during the day. Here the men would learn how to shoot their weapons and perform various maneuvers. Drill sessions lasted approximately two hours each.

One soldier described his days in the army like this: "The first thing in the morning is drill. Then drill, then drill again. Then drill, drill, a little more drill. Then drill, and lastly drill."

Other daily activities between drilling included cleaning the camp, building roads, digging trenches for latrines, and gathering wood for cooking and heating. Finding clean water was a constant goal. And always laundry.

They were fed fairly well at first. They were provided with at least 20 ounces of fresh or salt beef, or 12 ounces of salt pork, more than a pound of flour, and a vegetable, usually beans. Coffee, salt, vinegar, and sugar were provided as well. Supplies became limited when armies were moving fast and supply trains could not reach them in the field.

A typical scene of meal preparations for Civil War Negro soldiers

To escape the boredom, the men looked for recreational outlets. One letter writer stated, "There is some of the onerest men here that I ever saw, and the most swearing and card playing and fitin [fighting] and drunkenness that I ever saw at any place."

Minty's grandsons that she knew about were assigned menial tasks, such as cooking. The cooking was done on a campfire in large copper kettles, or they used sheet iron mess pans, something like a roasting pan.

The food was plain and simple. Once in a while they had fresh beef and vegetable soup. Salt beef was their stand-by. Sometimes they had slapjacks, which were flour made into bread. Each man had one of them or a pint of tea and five or six hard-tack (a three-inch square flat, bland cracker).

When in the field, soldiers saw little beef and few vegetables; they subsisted for the most part on salt pork, dried beans, corn bread, and hardtack—a flour-and-water biscuit often infested with maggots and weevils after storage. Outbreaks of scurvy were common due to a frequent lack of fresh fruits and vegetables.

By far, the most important staple in the minds of the soldiers was coffee. Men pounded the beans between rocks or crushed them with the butts of their rifles to obtain grounds with which to brew the strong drink. Although most Federals were well-supplied with coffee, the Confederates were often forced to make do with substitutes made from peanuts, peas, potatoes and chicory.

Most armies were forced at some point to live off the land. The Confederates, who fought mostly on home ground, tried harder to curb pillaging, preferring to request donations from townspeople rather than steal supplies or take them by force.

When not drilling or standing guard, the troops read, wrote letters to their loved ones, and played any game they could devise, including baseball, cards, boxing matches, and cockfights. One competition involved racing lice or cockroaches across a strip of canvas. As hard as most commanders attempted to control vice in camp, both gambling and drinking were rampant, especially after payday. And again, there was always laundry, as well as other chores.

Army regulations prohibited the purchase of alcohol by enlisted men, and soldiers who violated the rule were punished, but men on both sides found ways around it. Members of a Mississippi company got a half a gallon of whisky past the camp guards by concealing it in a hollowed- out watermelon; they then buried the melon beneath the floor of their tent and drank from it with a long straw. If they could not buy liquor, they made it. One Union recipe called for "bark juice, tar-water, turpentine, brown sugar, lamp oil, and alcohol."

In the winter when it was very cold, the soldier would take his mess pan outside, put a little dirt in it, go to the cook-shed and fill it nearly full of coals, carry it back to his tent and put another pan over it so the provost would not see the light. In this way his tent was heated and he kept warm.

One of the most difficult tasks assigned to the blacks was that of burying the dead. After a battle, whichever side won the field faced the overwhelming job of burying the dead. Usually groups of soldiers were assigned to burial details for this disagreeable task. The bodies in this next picture have been carried from where they fell and laid in a row for burial.

Soldiers buried by members of their own army generally received a decent burial. Many, who died on a field claimed by the enemy, were probably thrown into a ditch and covered with dirt. Some of the troops would be missing their footwear. Soldiers took them from the corpses when they gained control of a part of the field.

Veterans in the ranks knew what they were up against; before the fight, they sewed or pinned their names and addresses to their uniforms so their bodies could be

Dead Civil War soldiers awaiting burial

identified. Sometimes bodies lay in the open for a long time, or eroded out of their shallow graves, forcing workers to return and bury them again. The men in these burial details may have been escaped slaves, since many fugitives who fled to the Union lines were put to work for the army.

During battles black men were often placed in greater jeopardy than their white counterparts, and their mortality rates were correspondingly higher. Black soldiers generally expected to be killed if they were captured, and of those who were placed in Prisoner-of-War (POW) camps, only a few survived to be set free in March 1865. Wounded men were not given proper, if any, medical treatment, and the South refused to recognize black soldiers as POWs, instead treating them as insurgent slaves, so they were not included in prisoner exchanges.

At the start of the war, black men had rushed to enlist but were rejected because of a law that barred Negroes from bearing arms. This law was later abolished and blacks were allowed to serve in the artillery and infantry and performed all noncombatant support functions that sustain an army.

Bodies of soldiers needing to be reburied

Some families followed their loved ones to war.

Chapter Twenty-Three

Civil War:
Diseases and Medical Treatment

Minty worried about her grandsons. Whenever she heard of soldiers dying from sickness her heart would skip a beat. Could this be happening to her boys? She heard that yellow fever, cholera, typhoid, and similar contagious diseases invaded the camps and that they killed twice as many soldiers during the Civil War as wounds did. When an outbreak of other diseases, which were generally not fatal, occurred, an entire unit could be crippled. Except for epidemics, however, most military hospitals were filled with patients suffering from sexually related diseases.

TEARS THAT CHANGED A NATION

During the American Civil War the surgeon general reported that among the Union troops there were about 103,000 cases of gonorrhea and more than 73,000 cases of syphilis, with 155 deaths attributed to those causes. Confederate figures were probably comparable.

None of the treatments of the 1860's would have eradicated these diseases, so the men who became infected during their stints as soldiers could infect their wives or sweet-hearts upon returning home. There are no statistics on the number of women and subsequent children infected with venereal disease; however, considering the fact that Union physicians treated 170,000 cases of venereal disease, the figures must be staggering. One Civil War researcher estimated that one-third of the men who died in Union and Confederate veterans' homes were killed by the later stages of venereal disease. Due to the large number of camp followers, there were more cases of venereal diseases than of measles, mumps and tonsillitis together. [http:// www.mnwelldir.org/docs/history/civil_war.htm]

When not drinking or gambling, some men escaped the tedium of daily army life by enjoying "horizontal refreshments," as visiting prostitutes became known. Thousands of prostitutes thronged the cities in the war zones and clustered about the camps. By 1862, for instance, Washington, D.C., had 450 bordellos and at least 7,500 full- time prostitutes; Richmond, as the center of prostitution in the Confederacy, had about an equal number. Prostitution experienced its largest growth during 1861-1865 Some historians have speculated that this growth can be attributed to a depression, and a need for women to support themselves and families while their husbands were away at war. Some claimed that some women wanted to spread venereal disease to the opposing troops. Cities were not the only places of prostitution. Small towns located just outside the camps were most prominent, becoming overrun by the sex trade.

One soldier wrote home to his wife, "It is said that one house in every ten is a bawdy house—it is a perfect Sodom." (Sex in the American Civil War, Wikepedia)

Venereal disease among soldiers was prevalent and largely uncontrolled. About eight percent of the soldiers in the Union army were treated for venereal disease during the war and a great many cases were unreported; figures for the Confederacy are unavailable, but assumed to be about equal in proportion. With the invention of penicillin more than 70 years away, treating venereal disease with herbs and minerals such as pokeweed, elderberries, mercury, and zinc sulfate may have eased symptoms but did nothing to cure the disease.

The supply of whiskey was not as short as that of medicines. The so-called "moonshiners" of the mountains of North Carolina, Tennessee, Alabama and Georgia kept their stills, (often called gum-logs) running night and day, and could find a ready sale for all they produced. Surgical fevers disheartened the doctors. Four or five days after a wound operation, the patient would be recovering well, producing copious pus. Then suddenly the pus stopped, the wound dried, and the patient ran a terrific fever. Despite drugs, the patient would very likely be dead in three or four days. The diagnosis was blood poisoning.

Erysipelas also affected both armies. During the Civil War, there were many different kinds of camp followers. Some of these included nurses hired by the government or just volunteering out of compassion, wives who cooked and did laundry for their husbands, and "ladies of entertainment". Low wages during the inflationary war period inspired many women, especially of the lower class, to take up prostitution, including women who were barely older than what we today consider to be children. Also, many female slaves were sent into the camps to provide financial support for the plantations. Even the Federal Government set up houses of prostitution. This brought into the camps diseases that many soldiers, out of shame or embarrassment, tried to conceal their infections or treat them on their own.

One might wonder why the churches did not speak out against this curse of prostitution, but this was not a topic that was discussed openly because of the embarrassment.

Remedies for these diseases included poke roots and berries, sassafras, and wild sarsaparilla. None of these were effective. Mercury, however, actually did provide some relief from pain, but no permanent positive effects. The surgeons were in the dark as to how to treat this affliction, but it was noted that if iodine was painted on the edges of a wound, its further extension was stopped. Civil War surgeons had not only iodine but carbolic acid as well, and a long list of "disinfectants" such as bichloride of mercury, sodium hypochlorite, and other agents. The trouble was that the wound was allowed to become a raging inferno before disinfectants were tried.

Many soldiers, when sent home, carried their disease with them to wives and girlfriends. Little, if anything, has been recorded as to the heartache and suffering this brought to families because of the shame associated with it. Over 100,000 Union soldiers suffered this and probably a like number of Confederate soldiers. Also, adding to the heartache and pain, left behind were the thousands of mulatto babies who would be brought up with all the injustices faced by the blacks, regardless of their appearances as Caucasian, with light skin and hair and blue eyes.

[In 1850, the census records indicated whether an individual were white, black, or mulatto. This ended in 1880]

CIVIL WAR DISEASES AND TREATMENT

Documented pneumonia took the lives of almost 20,000 Federal and 19,000 Confederate soldiers; while smallpox killed 1,000 soldiers in three months in one Virginia hospital. Scarlet fever and measles occasionally caused a death.

Foul drinking water led to diarrhea, dysentery, typhoid and pneumonia, which caused hundreds of thousands of deaths. The Civil War soldier might be considered unfortunate in the fact that when he entered the war, the killing power of weaponry was being brought to a new peak of efficiency and the science of medicine was incredibly imperfect.

When he fought, he was likely to be hurt pretty badly, and when he stayed in camp, he lived under conditions that were very likely to make him sick. In either case he had almost no chance of getting the kind of medical treatment which for a generation or so later would be routine. About half of the deaths from disease during the Civil War were caused by intestinal disorders, mainly typhoid fever, diarrhea, and dysentery. The remainder died from pneumonia and tuberculosis.

The camp conditions brought on much of the sickness. Each company was supposed to have a sink, a trench eight feet deep and two feet wide, onto which six inches of earth were to be put each evening. Some regiments, at first, dug no sinks. In other cases the men, disgusted by the sights and odors around the sinks, went off into open spaces around the edge of the camp. The infestation of flies that followed was inevitable; as were the diseases and bacteria they spread to the men and their rations. Complaints of loose bowels brought long lines of soldiers to the sick call. The medical officer attributed all these cases to eating bad or badly cooked food, lumping all the cases together as one disease, while in fact, there were many other causes. The Union Army alone blamed the disease for

50,000 deaths, a sum larger than that ascribed to "killed in action." It was even more lethal in the Confederate Army.

The diets of both armies were deplorably high in calories and low in vitamins. Fruits and fresh vegetables were notable by their absence, and especially so when the army was in the field. The food part of the ration was fresh or preserved beef, salt pork, navy beans, coffee, and hardtack (large, thick crackers, usually stale and often inhabited by weevils). When troops were not fighting, many created funds to buy fruits and vegetables in the open market. More often they foraged in the countryside, with fresh food a valuable part of the booty.

As for medicines with which to treat the ailing soldiers, druggists of the South had either to manufacture what they could from native barks and leaves and herbs and roots or purchase at the Southern ports such supplies as the blockade runners brought in that were not intended for the government. Disinfectants included red-oak bark added to the water, a weak solution of bicarbonate of soda, slippery elm and wahoo root bark, and sometimes a solution of common salt. Extreme pain medication included poppy heads, nightshade, and stramonium. Fevers called for substitutes for quinine. Strong teas were made from boneset, butterfly root, pleurisy root, mandrake, Virginia snake root, and yellow root, among others. Whatever the ailment seemed to be, knowledge of the curative effects of herbs, which grew in abundance in the hills and dales, was put to use as substitutes for opiates.

In the event of an engagement, the assistant surgeon and one or more detailed men, laden with lint, bandages, opium pills and morphine, and whiskey and brandy, would establish an "advance" or dressing station just beyond musket fire from the battle. Stretcher-bearers went forward to find the wounded and, if the latter could not walk, to carry them to the dressing station. The assistant surgeon gave the wounded man a stout drink of liquor, expecting it to counteract shock, and then perhaps gave him an opium pill or dusted or rubbed morphine into the wound. After removing foreign bodies, he packed the wound with lint, bandaged it, and applied a splint if it seemed advisable. The walking wounded then started for the field hospital, officially the regiment hospital tent. There, lying on clumps of hay or bare ground, the wounded awaited their turn on the operating table. There was usually little shouting, groaning, or clamor because the wounded were quieted by shock and the combination of liquor and opiate. It was an eerie scene, with a mounting pile of amputated limbs, perhaps five feet high.

Everything about the operation was septic. The surgeon operated in a blood, and often pus-stained coat. He might hold his lancet in his mouth. If he dropped an instrument or sponge, he picked it up, rinsed it in cold water, and continued work. When loose pieces of bone and tissue had been removed, the wound would be packed with moist lint or raw cotton, unsterilized, and bandaged with wet, unsterilized bandages. The bandages were to be kept wet, the patient was to be kept as quiet as possible, and he was to be given small but frequent doses of whiskey and possibly quinine.

Transporting the sick and the wounded presented another problem. Ambulance wagons, or wagons especially designed for the transport of sick and wounded, had not been in use in the armies of the United States until a year or so before the outbreak of the War of the Rebellion. Transport carts, army wagons, ox teams, in fact anything that could be made available for the purpose, had been employed. The wounded could not be transported in them, on account of the roughness of the road; sometimes they would be brought a part of the way on litters between two horses."

[The bloody Civil War claimed 620,000 lives—more than World Wars I and II, Korea, and Vietnam combined.]

Gen. Hooker did much to forward medical knowledge by his thoughtful introduction of "ladies of entertainment" to the camps at Nashville, which subsequently became the syphilis center of America. Because of that, much scramble was made to experiment with sulpha and other remedies that led to antibiotics. In every cloud, perhaps a silver lining. They knew what STD was, just not too much about its cure.

[Many soldiers injured in the Civil War depended on the habit forming opium for pain. This drug could be smoked, chewed, and swallowed in liquid form. Many came home addicted. Dr. Frank E. Marsh of Quincy, Michigan built a national reputation for successfully treating this opium problem. He set up a clinic at the corner of 46 W. Chicago and Arnold Streets where he offered specialized counseling and treatment. He helped thousands of people, both local and out of state. He was known as the great opium healer.]

Savage Station, Virginia. Union field hospital after the battle of June 27, 1828.

Chapter Twenty-Four

Letters from Camp

Even more pervasive than boredom, gambling, or venereal disease was homesickness. Men spent more time writing letters and hoping to receive them than any other leisure activity. Furloughs were rarely granted, and most soldiers had few opportunities to spend extended periods of time away from the army. Federal troops were often stationed too far from home to have time to get home, while Southern armies, short of manpower, needed every available soldier to fight. For better or worse, Civil War soldiers were forced to call camp home for the duration of their terms of service.

Minty often thought about the camp life of her grandsons. She tried to picture what the camps looked like. She eagerly looked forward to letters from them, always hoping for scraps of information.

Time spent in an army camp during the Civil War might be a day, a week, or several weeks. In between skirmishes and battles the soldiers had little to do other than the daily chores and drills. Some played cards or gambled, some sang, anything to defeat boredom and combat loneliness. Many wrote letters to wives, girlfriends, or others. Many others just hoped for a letter. Following are excerpts taken from letters written by soldiers, both Yankees and Confederates, to loved ones and friends. Since letters are one of the best sources of information about what life was like as a Civil War soldier, reading these will help one to understand their experiences, their feelings, their loneliness, and their thoughts.

A Confederate camp

A Union Camp

Letter Excerpts

Misspellings and grammatical errors as written

"I am also letting you know that we again have sent a letter to A. Plugger. I have to keep 15 dollars.

This time I did not dare enclose 20 dollars, because you don't know t happen, because I don't want to starve as long as I am here. I cannot understand that you did not receive a letter from me for a month, because most of the time I do write week, if not more than that."

"The weather is hot here I could go barefooted and not half try Contrabands are as thick as thick I could hire hundreds ted them I have seen a good many negro soldiers they look sweet They put on a heap of style."

"Dear I could not even buy me a sheet of paper in Winchester to write to you. There is none to be bought. The boys are writing on paper that they have captured on the battle field. Whenever you write to me you must send me a blank sheet of paper in your letter"

"I now sit down to try to write you a few lines as we have lately come off of a very hard expedition of marching and fighting. We was skirmishing about 15 days all together and then after that 10 days hard marching, day and night both

and very scarce of rations but it is all over now We are in camp close to the Mississippi River. It has been just one week since we come here and we moved camp today. We was about a quarter of a mile from the river and today [Sunday] we moved down close to the river so we would be handy to water. I went out this forenoon to get some brush to make a shade for my mess and it was about a mile to the woods where we went to get brush and it was very tiresome work and when we come back we got our dinners and then went out to get some green corn to make beds, we don't mind that in this country. We just use it the same as we do anything else for anything that we want it for."

"The weather here is very hot and dry. We have not had any rain of any account since the 23rd of April but the river has been very high but is falling now. We have fixed up Camp as if we was going to stay here some time but we don't know anything about it. I have a great deal of work to do now for I have to attend to beating all the calls. We have ten drummers and ten fifers and I am put at the head of them all and have to boss them all and that is what makes the work. Our drum major has never come back yet since we have been back and don't know whether he will or not."

"the long to be remembered field of bloodshed and slaughter. … There many a poor fell(own) lost their life for their country and their people"

"Well Spence I am very sorry to hear of _____ death for he was a good old dog …Will has had the Yellow Jaundice and now he has got the Mumps. There is several more of the company got them."

"May 23, 1862 Roller, MD
Dear mother,

I tuck this time unite to informed you that was well and hope these fief lines will find you all well. We are in roller County. Yesterday we went 40 miles back to flat top mountain. If we would state on the east river twenty four hours longer we wooed aside Richmond."

"Three thousand come in behind us and the happened to be too Companies of the Soave was there and a fief Cavalry. The fought them half away. The rebels had three thousand against too hindered. The two Soave Companies charged on them and tuck won Cannon from them and the saw that the coo dent holed the Canon and the spiked the Cannon.

We come out in the evening and louder to surrounded them. The was six thousand rite behind us and then the was after our team of horses but the horses ran away acumen back to us.

Our Cornel he bet ahondard dollars that the war wood stop in thirty days. I wish hit was over now for iam tiered astayen here in the servise.

I hant got A Crutch of fear from no body Sence I left home Ia About eight hundred milds from home Jane I dont no how to write if I git A letter I wood no better how to write Jane tell brother that I am A looking for A letter from him thay Say that the Yankes is Advansing on richmon A gin we hav to go and defend it we A folling back o of east tennessee Jane we saw a bad time A marching threw the snow & rain thay are A feeding us on oats & rye & wheat mus-togather & it not boiled the chaf & brand is all in it Giv my lov and best respects to all friends I must Close So no more at present Only remains your truly husband until death

Write soon Good By Wen this you See remember Me"

"Our men had a big fight last Monday at Leesburg a little town about twenty miles from here. We whipped them again and that badly the _____ of killed, wounded, and taken prisoners on the Yankee side is said to be at least 1200 about 600 of the North wer taken prisoners. 100 killed and 300 wounded besides several hundred drowned while crossing."

"We had another great battle Sunday, it commenced at 6 o'clock and ended at 6 o'clock, it was the hardest battle ever fought in America. They had 10 to our one—we conquered them, we lost about 800 in killed and wounded. The Yankees lost about 5,000 and we took 1,300 prisoners and 125 horses, baggage wagons and 64 pieces of cannon besides a great many things … I had to be up all night to guard the wounded—it was the saddest thing I ever saw to hear the moans of the wounded and dying. I saw the surgeons operating on them, it made me shed tears to see how they suffered, some had to have both of their arms cut off and some their legs. I saw all the surgeons operations, it was a distressing sight to see them how they suffered …"

"James has just been here with a telegraphic dispatch of the Death of Father. Just as I had written the last sentence in a letter to Father. James tried to obtain a furlough for us to attend the Funeral but it was beyond the power of our Col to grant it as he had orders not to grant any furloughs on any account …"

"We ran out 3 or 4 miles yesterday expecting a fight but we came across no rebels the Majors orderly saw fifteen rebel Cavalry thats generally our luck we go out cheering and in the best of spirits and come back cussing and swearing ..."

"Sometimes on the skirmish line we and the Rebs. make agreement not to fire at each other and meet and talk together trade coffee for tobacco, then go back to our respective post and commence firing at each other. Don't this look horrible, as it were brother against brother trying to kill each other."

"There were 64 killed and wounded in the Regt. 10 were killed some have died there wounds being mortal. Our color bearer was amongst the killed. Sergt. Botts was his name. The Rebs. suffered severely. I passed over the battlefield this morning they lay in heaps over the ground. Our men were busily burying them this morning as decently as circumstances would admit. Our men were also decently interred this forenoon, Chaplain Stillwell held religious services thus we paid the last sad rights to our deceased comrades. It is horrible that man will so continue to butcher one another in such a manner. The enemy left the field with their dead and wounded behind. We brought in several wounded Rebs. Never have I seen human limbs lying scattered over the ground like so many beef limbs.
Some three or four hundred prisoners were captured some came in and gave themselves up. Say they are tired of fighting. Some are in earnest however, even some of the wounded say if they get well and are exchanged they will try us again."

"You would be surprised to see me marching along; the sun pouring down, an awful heavy knapsack on my back, haversack full, canteen, gun, and cartridge box with forty rounds in not feel my knapsack for two or three miles after I got the letter. All our troops are coming back; I think the object is to meet the rebels, who left their fortifications and intended, it is supposed, to get back by a round-about way, and cut off our supplies; but I guess Rosecrans is equal t o them."

"I was on guard the other night—it was raining hard and the mud was awful. It stopped raining about 10 P.M. I was on the first relief—George Harris and I were next to the Colonel's quarters. The cook had left a fire there, also a bucket. We laid our guns across the bucket and sat by the fire, both wondering what our parents would think to see us there at midnight watching our lonely beat. I am quite well. We have had no long marches lately. The days are very warm and nights very cold; we have to find winter quarters soon. Osc. and I sleep very comfortably. We lay a rubber blanket on the ground, then a woolen one; we take off our pants and blouses, lie down, and cover up with a woolen and rubber.

"I often think of home, and wonder what the folks are doing there. We heard that the 35th was in Cynthiana. I hope there will be a move forward soon, to do something; it seems as if the war was too slow. Perhaps we will winter in Ohio; I hope so."" More men came from the hospital last night, so that guard duty will not be so heavy. They report a great deal of sickness and many deaths. The typhoid fever is prevalent. Some of our boys are very sick. It seems that those swho go instead of going to the hospital, get well the sooner. The idea is quite prevalent that we will winter in Ohio-Camp Dennison."

TEARS THAT CHANGED A NATION

Some, with so much time on their hands, took great pains with their letter writing. The writer of the following letter drew an intricate border around his letter, as well as setting it into poetry. This individual, Daniel S. Ferguson, is said to have at one time become separated from his unit in Georgia and spent the winter in a corn shock, coming out only at night to forage for food and water. This letter belongs to the family of Darrel Butters, the great grandson of Daniel Ferguson who is buried in the cemetery in Litchfield, Michigan.

The letter is transcribed here:

Camp at Columbia Tennessee January 1st, 1865

Dearest Wife I Still Remember With A Husband's Aching Heart, How It Filled My Heart With Sorrow When We Two Were Called To Part

Oft I Feel Within My Breast As The Shades Of Night Appear Purest Love And Fond Affection For My Own My Absent Dear

Though I'm But A Ordley Sergt Gone To Fill My Countyrs Call

All My Trust Is In The Savior Let Me Stand Or Let Me Fall

When I Get Your Welcome Letters As In Dixie Land I Roam And You Speak Of Our Dear Love How It Makes Me Sigh For Home

How I Love The Sacred Altar Where We Used To Kneel In Prayer

What A Comfort What A Blessing O I Wish That I Was There

But I Hope The Day Is Darkning Which Will Close This Bloody Strife And Ear Long To Have The Pleasuare Of Embracing My Dear Wife

Let Us Then My Dear Companion Humbly At His Footstool Live Striving To Obtain The Treasur Which The Lord Will Surely Give

Then If We Are Only Faithful

To The Lord Our Truest Friend Safe Will We Rise To Realms Of Glory Where Our Bliss Will Never End.

There is only one known letter written by a black soldier during the Civil War, therefore, the entire letter is given:

"We have had a hard time for the last week, today one week ago, we left Bacon Creek for Green River; arrived at and crossed the river that night and camped next to the battle killed there, and saw where Col. Terry, Col. of the Texas Rangers was killed. The rebels had three car loads of dead sent here, and would not let anybody know how many there was killed.

We left Green River on Thursday morning about daylight, and came about twenty miles, and then stopped for the night. We thought we would not put up our tents, so we laid on the ground, but Lieut. H. and myself fixed a shed with rails in a fence corner. The next morning everything was covered up with snow, and we would go around to a pile of snow, kick it and somebody would jump up. On Friday, Feb. 14th, we came on a gallop and hired wagons to bring the knapsacks for the infantry so we could hurry up as we was told the rebels was going to burn the town and leave it, so we hurried as fast as we could, but when we got here the bridge across Barren River was burning, so we could not cross, and Capt. Loomis planted his artillery on this side and commenced firing at ten minutes before 12 o'clock; they fired at an engine that was standing on the track by the depot, one ball passed through two brick walls of the depot, and there were five more locomotives ready to start out, but they then started with one, and left one cannon, and then they went over the the hills and left some of the Texas Rangers to burn the town, they burned the depot and engine house with a lot of muskets, pistols, sabres and tents; they burned nearly all the business part of the town, a large pork house full of pork and bacon.

We had to just stand there and look at it burn, as we could not cross the river, but one of the citizens told us of a ferry that was down the river two miles, at a mill; some of the infantry crossed that night and we crossed the next morning, the town was nearly in ruins.

We went out on the Nashville Pike on Saturday morning about five miles, but did not find anybody, but saw a railroad bridge burning. We came back and took possession of a livery station for our horses, and we are quartered in a large three story hotel. We are having very hard times here, we have to do all the scouting, and most of the picket duty. I have slept but one night since last Saturday week ago, and am almost played out-I expect we will leave here tomorrow for Nashville and then we will be ready to march through to New Orleans.

I expect before this reaches you we will be on the road to Nashville. Some of the boys went out scouting last Saturday afternoon, and returned late last night with a prisoner and his horse. They saw a regiment 17 miles from here and had to retreat. We took 5 prisoners on our route here. We lost nary a man. "

C. FAILOR, Co. A 4th Reg. Ohio Cavalry

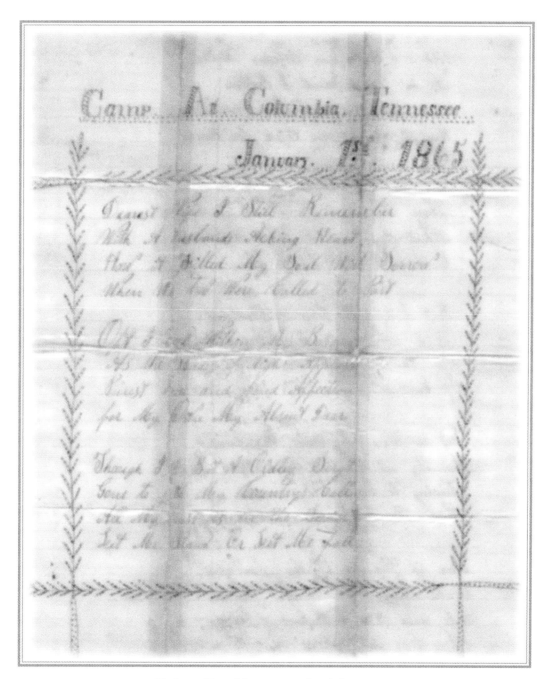

The letter of Daniel S. Ferguson as described on page 156

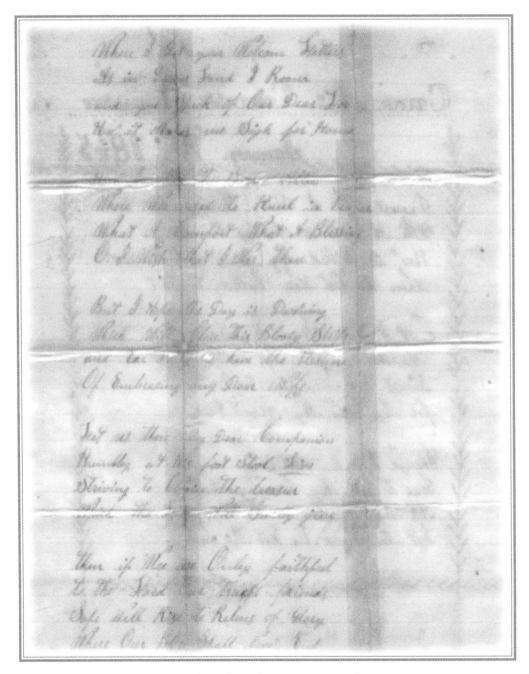

The letter of Daniel S. Ferguson continued

Chapter Twenty-Five

Animals in the *Civil War*

M inty realized that animals played an important role in the Civil War. Some of these included animals used for mascots or pets, such as dogs, cats, donkeys, bears, eagles, pelicans, and even camels. They traveled along with Union and Confederate armies into the thick of battle, providing companionship, comfort, and entertainment along the way. General Lee even had a pet hen.

Dogs were by far the most popular army mascots. Besides being used for companionship, most dogs could be trained to help their masters' forage for food, carry supplies, do tracking, or even search for dead and wounded soldiers when the need arose. Man's best friend, indeed. Also, pigeons were valuable for use in sending messages.

Horses, however, were another story. Although few people realize it, the horse was the backbone of the Civil War. Without them there could have been no war. Horses moved guns and ambulances, carried generals and messages, and usually gave all they had. The total number of horses and mules killed in the Civil War mounts up to more than one million. In the beginning of the war, more horses were being killed than men. The number killed at the Battle of Gettysburg alone totaled around 1,500. The field artillery of the Civil War was designed to be mobile. When Union or Confederate troops marched across country, the guns moved with them. During battle, the guns were moved to assigned positions and then were switched from place to place, pulled back or sent forward as fortune

Loomis Battery, Coldwater, Michigan

demanded. The field batteries went galloping off to support an advance or repel an attack. When they withdrew, they contested the field as they went. Movement was everything. The guns could fulfill their essential function only when they could be moved where they were most needed. At the time of the Civil War, such movement required draft animals–horses, mules, or oxen. Mules were excellent at pulling heavy loads, but they were not used in pulling the guns and caissons of the field artillery.

No animal liked to stand under fire. In the fury of battle, horses would shy and rear and flash their hooves; but mules carried their protests to the outer limits. When exposed to fire, mules would buck and kick and roll on the ground, entangling harnesses and becoming impossible to control.

An exception to the rule against using mules was their role in carrying small mountain howitzers. These guns were light enough to be broken down, with the component parts carried on the backs of pack animals. They had been developed for use in country that was mountainous and heavily wooded, with only trails or wretched roads. Strong, surefooted animals were needed, and mules were the obvious choice. The superiority of mules in rough country outweighed their notorious contrariness under fire.

Plodding oxen obviously were not well suited for hauling field artillery, since rapid movement was often needed. Oxen were strong. Their name is synonymous with strength and endurance, but they were too slow. Nevertheless, oxen were sometimes pressed into service during the Civil War. Proper and adequate care of artillery horses was essential. If they were weakened by neglect, they could not long survive the rigors of active campaigning. Good commanders were aware of this and issued orders aimed at improving the care of the animals. Those guilty of neglect of battery horses were to be punished. No artillery horses were to be ridden except by designated artillerymen. The chief of artillery was empowered to arrest and bring to trial any man using a horse other than in battery service.

When a battery came to a halt during a march, every opportunity should be taken advantage of to cut grass, wheat, or oats, and extraordinary care to be taken of the horses upon which everything depends.

Feeding, of course, was a critical part of the horse's care. The daily ration prescribed for an artillery horse was fourteen pounds of hay and twelve pounds of grain, usually oats, corn or barley. The amount of grain and hay needed by any particular battery depended on the number of horses that battery had at the time. It varied almost from day to day, but it was always enormous. The horses of the battery had to be fed each day, whether the battery moved or not. During the Civil War, an artillery battery might sit in the same place for weeks at a time, and yet consume thousands of pounds of hay and grain each day.

Artillery horses represented only a small number of the animals that had to be fed by the military. Besides the horses with the artillery, horses used by the cavalry, and horses and mules used to pull supply wagons and ambulances, there were also thousands of saddle horses carrying officers and couriers. Eight hundred thousand pounds of forage and grain were needed daily to feed the horses and mules. Since a wagon ordinarily carried one ton, the animals' daily food allowance required four hundred wagonloads each day.

Sometimes the men were granted "horse furloughs". Those who had nearby homes were allowed to return home if each took a horse with him.

The furloughed soldier was expected to feed and care for the horse, and when spring arrived, he was to return to the battery with the horse.

Water for the horses was a problem that demanded an adequate solution every day. While in camp, a battery would discover the nearest creek or pond and routinely water the horses there. On the march, water had to be found at the end of each day. If the water was any distance, as it often was, the timing of the watering was critical. The guns were immobile if the horses were absent. Usually, only half the horses would be sent to water at any one time. This meant that in an emergency some movement might be achieved, but with only half the horses present, the battery was at a distinct disadvantage.

In spite of the care given to artillery horses, the animals still perished at an astounding rate. Many died of disease or were put to death because of exhaustion. Many more were killed alongside their battery mates in battle.

One tactic used in attacking a battery was to shoot down the horses attached to it. If the battery horses were killed or disabled, moving the guns back to safety was an impossible task. But horses could take much punishment. They were difficult to bring down, and once down were difficult to keep down, even with the impact of the large- caliber Minie bullets.

By far the greatest number of horses were lost to disease and exhaustion. The most prevalent disease in the battery was glanders, which claimed 45 horses. Glanders, a highly contagious disease that affects the skin, nasal passages and respiratory tract of horses and mules, was also called farcy or nasal gleet in wartime reports.

The horses were worked hard and long, but it had to be so. A battery racing to catch up with a retreating enemy or to gain a position of advantage had no room for gentle treatment. The stakes were high, and the horses paid the price. The alternative might be defeat. A man on a long, hot march, pushed beyond what his body could bear, might drop out temporarily and catch up with his company later. Horses had no such choice. Harnessed to the limbers, they pulled until they fell or, as happened in most instances, until they harmed their bodies beyond healing, and then were shot.

Mud or dust seemed to plague every movement of troops. Of the two, mud was the greater problem for the artillery. Mud often made movement impossible. Sinking below their axles in holes full of clinging muck, guns and caissons could be moved only with superhuman effort, the men pushing at the wheels and extra horses pulling on the traces. Sometimes guns were simply abandoned to the mud.

Horses and mules, which were essential for cavalry, artillery, and transportation units as well as for officers' mounts, were not the only animal life to be seen in the army camps of the Civil War. Despite orders to the contrary many pets were seen as companions to the homesick young men as well as the officers. Some of these included dogs, cats, squirrels, raccoons, and other wildlife. One regiment had a bald eagle that was carried on its own perch next to the regiment flags. General Lee had a chicken which furnished him with a fresh egg every day. The most popular pet was the dog. Whatever the pet, they were morale boosters. The navy used cats on the ships to help with rat and mice infestation.

Many are the stories that could be told of the famous horse and dog heroes of the Civil War. One particularly interesting story involves a pig. One day a German soldier brought back with him on his return from a furlough, a poor, thin little pig. His regiment, the 74th Pennsylvania, was just embarking for the North, where it was ordered to join the 10th Corps, and he could not take the pig back with him, so he gave it to our colonel. That pig grew to be the pet of the camp, and was the special care of the drummer boys, who taught him many tricks; and so well did they train him that every day at practice and dress parade, his pigship would march out with them, keeping perfect time with their music. The drummers would often disturb the devotions by riding this pig into the midst of evening praise meeting, and many were the complaints made to the colonel, but he was always very lenient towards the boys, for he knew they only did this for mischief. They would never forget the fun they had in camp with "Piggie."

And, of course, there's always Old Sam! He was the hero horse from Coldwater, Michigan, the only one of 200 horses from there to survive the war. Old Sam was the favorite of the Loomis Battery of Michigan.

Chapter Twenty-Six

Stephen Foster
and the Civil War

Another person crossing the stage of Minty O'Banion's life during the Antebellum and Civil War years was Stephen Foster, the acknowledged "father of American music". Although Minty had no connection with him personally, she was very familiar with his music which had been in existence since before 1846. Although, she may well have been in his presence through her ties to Harriette Beecher Stowe.

Foster was born in Pennsylvania on July 4, 1826, the ninth of ten children. He detested school and was poorly educated, but he was an avid reader and showed great interest in music. He taught himself to play the guitar, flute, clarinet, violin, and the piano. Although Foster never formally studied composition, by the age of fourteen he was writing songs.

His first published song, *Open Thy Lattice Love*, came out when he was eighteen. As a teen, Foster enjoyed the friendship of young men and women from some of Pittsburgh's most prosperous and respectable families. They often met at the Foster home where one of their principal activities was singing, with Stephen acting first as song leader and then composer. Some of his earliest songs were written for this group.

In 1846, when he was twenty, he moved to Cincinnati to work as a bookkeeper for his brother at his steamboat firm. While there he had several songs published. His first big hit was *Oh! Susanna*. The forty-niners and others heading west picked up the song and it is still identified with travel west years later. He returned to Pennsylvania in 1850, married, and continued writing songs. By this time he already had twelve compositions in print. It was said that when inspired he could dash off perfect masterpieces. Many of his songs expressed sentiment of antebellum South.

Although many of his songs had Southern themes, Foster never lived in the South and visited it only once, by river- boat voyage (on his brother Dunning's steam boat, the Millinger) down the Mississippi to New Orleans, during his honeymoon in 1852.

Foster sold minstrel songs to stage performers, but they were instructed not to mock slaves, but rather to get their audiences to feel compassion for them. It is said that African Americans liked his music because it was just plain good. His songs were different and separate from the truly racist songs of the period. He had said that he sought to "build up taste among refined people by making words to their taste, instead of the trashy and really offensive words which belong to some songs of that order." He tried to reform black-face minstrelsy. His intention was to write the people's music, using images and a musical vocabulary that would be widely understood by all groups. Foster worked very hard at writing, sometimes taking several months to craft and polish the words, melody, and accompaniment of a song before sending it off to a publisher. His sketchbook shows that he often labored over the smallest details, the right prepositions, even where to include or remove a comma from his lyrics.

His music sought to humanize the characters in his songs, to have them care for one another, and to convey a sense that all people share the same longings and needs for family and home. Foster may have been encouraged by his boyhood friend, Charles Shiras, abolitionist leader in Pennsylvania who launched an abolitionist newspaper, and probable acquaintance of those abolitionists in Cincinnati area.

Foster's *My Old Kentucky Home* was inspired by the most popular American novel of the nineteenth century—Harriet Beecher Stowe's *Uncle Tom's Cabin*. Both works lament the loss of a home in Kentucky. This fact showed that Foster did not justify nor glorify slavery. As much as she hated slavery, Harriet Beecher Stowe's view of the South was not all that different from Stephen Foster's. [Remember Harriet gained much of her information for her novel from Minty and Lewis O'Banion.] *My Old Kentucky Home* is the official state song of Kentucky, adopted by the General Assembly on March 19, 1928, and *Old Folks at Home* is the official state song of Florida, designated in 1935.

Although Abraham Lincoln was certainly exaggerating when he called Mrs. Stowe the little lady who started the big war, *Uncle Tom's Cabin* did hasten the war by fueling abolitionist passions. Nevertheless, the Southern whites depicted in that novel are generally good people, who are themselves victimized by an unjust institution.

The humble dwelling referred to in the title of Stowe's novel is a slave cabin on a plantation in Kentucky. Uncle Tom is forced to leave his old Kentucky home and his loving family when his otherwise indulgent owner, Mr. Shelby, falls into debt and is forced to liquidate some of his more valuable human assets. The speaker in Foster's song is a slave, who could very well be Uncle Tom. Like Old Black Joe, he begins by remembering the idyllic home he has lost. *My Old Kentucky Home* chorus is on the next page.

Foster ignored the American Civil War for a long time. He claimed to have nothing to do with that, because he didn't believe in the explanation, that this war was waged for the liberation of the slaves. However, during the War, he wrote several songs relating to it. Those written included *That's What's the Matter*, written after the slaughter at Shiloh, *Willie Has Gone to the War*, *When This Dreadful War Is Ended*, and *The Battle Cry for Freedom*.

Foster also composed dignified parlor music, especially for middle-aged women, as well as instrumental music, including the Social Orchestra, a collection of 73 arrangements for flute, piano, violin and other instruments. Probably his most famous parlor piece was *Jeanie with the Light Brown Hair*, written for his wife. He was not well known to the general public during his lifetime as he did not perform music professionally, but he did perform at social gatherings. He composed more than 200 works in his lifetime.

My Old Kentucky Home

Weep no more my lady
Oh! weep no more today!
We will sing one song for the old Kentucky home,
For the Old Kentucky Home far away.
The sun shines bright in the old Kentucky home, 'Tis summer, the people are gay;
The corn-top's ripe and the meadow's in the bloom,
While the birds make music all the day.
The young folks roll on the little cabin floor,
All merry, all happy and bright;
By 'n' by Hard Times comes a-knocking at the door,
Then my old Kentucky home, goodnight.
They hunt no more for the possum and the coon, On meadow, the hill and the shore,
They sing no more by the glimmer of the moon, On the bench by the old cabin door.
The day goes by like a shadow o'er the heart, With sorrow, where all was delight,
The time has come when the people have to part,
Then my old Kentucky home, goodnight.
The head must bow and the back will have to bend, Wherever the people may go;
A few more days, and the trouble all will end,
In the field where the sugar-canes grow;
A few more days for to tote the weary load, No matter, 'twill never be light;
A few more days till we totter on the road, Then my old Kentucky home, goodnight.

In 1857, in order to pay off his debts, he sold all rights to his song catalog to his publisher. He never caught up with his debts, but his publisher became very wealthy. He continued to write in order to exist in a hotel in New York until an accident in which he was burned by a lamp caused him to fall and strike his head. He died three days later in the hospital on January 13, 1864. Stephen Foster, possibly the best known song writer was not yet thirty-eight years old. In his pocket were thirty-eight cents and a scrap of paper that read "dear friends and gentle people."

Chapter Twenty-Seven

Lincoln's Assassination

The War was over. The joy of a homecoming of two grandsons for Minty's family was deeply over shadowed by the death of her grandson who had been killed at the Crater Battle of Petersburg. Even greater sorrow came at news of President Lincoln's assassination on April 14, 1865.

A crushing blow! Just five days after General Lee surrendered his Southern Army to General Grant at the McLean house near the Appomatox Courthouse.

John Wilkes Booth planned and carried out the assassination of Lincoln, a part of a larger conspiracy, while Lincoln was watching the play, Our American Cousin with his wife, Mary Todd Lincoln, at the Ford Theater in Washington, D.C.

Lincoln died early the next morning. Booth's plan had been to kidnap Lincoln and deliver him to the Confederate Army, to be held until the North agreed to resume prisoner exchange.

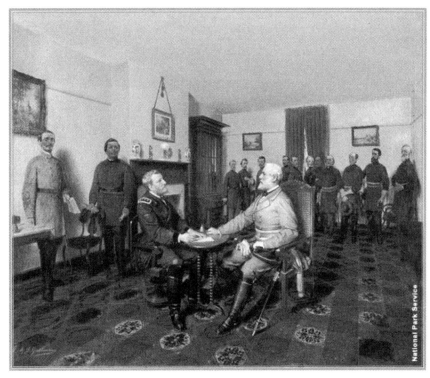

This painting hung in the Lewis Art Gallery in Coldwater, MI General Lee Surrenduring to General Grant

Lincoln had told several others three days earlier that he had had a dream about his being assassinated and that it had bothered him ever since.

The contents of Lincoln's pockets included two pairs of spectacles, a chamois lens cleaner, an ivory and silver pocketknife, a large white Irish linen handkerchief, slightly used, with "A. Lincoln" embroidered in red, a gold quartz watch fob without a watch, a new silk-lined leather wallet containing a pencil, a Confederate five-dollar bill, and news clippings of unrest in the Confederate Army, emancipation in Missouri, the Union party platform of 1864, and an article on the presidency by John Bright.

THE ASSASSINATION OF PRESIDENT LINCOLN.

AT FORD'S THEATRE WASHINGTON, D.C. APRIL 14TH 1865.

Published by Currier & Ives, 152 Nassau St New York

Map of Lincoln's Funeral Train Route

Lincoln's funeral train was dubbed "The Lincoln Special". His portrait was fastened to the front of the train above the cattle guard. Approximately 300 people accompanied his body on the 1,654 mile journey as it traveled through 180 cities and seven different states. Lincoln's son Robert also was on the train, as was the body of his son Willie which had been disinterred so that he could be buried alongside his father.

As the train traveled, scheduled stops were made. At each stop, Lincoln's coffin was taken off the train, placed on an elaborate horse-drawn hearse and led by solemn procession to a public building for viewing. In

Philadelphia, his body lay in state on the east wing of Independence Hall where the Declaration of Independence had been signed. The cities of Pittsburg and Cincinnati were omitted in favor of Chicago. The map below shows the route of the train from Washington D.C. to Springfield, Illinois. A disappointed Minty did not get to pay respects to her beloved president on his funeral train.

Memories of the death of another beloved president flooded Minty's eyes with tears. President Washington and now President Lincoln. How Minty thanked God that her own General Grant had escaped the assassin's bullet.

Chapter Twenty-Eight

The Freedmen's Society

With the war clouds hanging over everyone and slaves being set free by Lincoln, Minty hungered for any news about her Kentucky family. Many bloody battles were fought in Kentucky and Tennessee. Many of the freed slaves flocked within the Union lines as the armies advanced through Tennessee on the way to Memphis. New problems for the freedmen had arisen, and some of her family might be involved. Before the Emancipation and as the Union armies gathered in Kentucky and Tennessee, many of the slaveholders fled further south, taking their ablebodied slaves and leaving women and children, and the aged and sick ones behind to take care of themselves. These slaves were left with nothing as the armies consumed everthing. Thousands gathered within Union lines and were sent to various points up the river. Some were left on the wharf in Cincinnati with no food nor shelter. Blacks already living in the area helped as many as they could

Minty knew that Levi Coffin was busily traveling into the South drumming up support for the needs of these poor slaves who were left in a suffering condition. The Freedmen's Society was founded in 1861 during the Civil War, supported chiefly by the Congregational, Presbyterian, and Methodist churches in the North. It organized a supply of teachers to set up and teach in schools in the South so that Freedmen could be educated as teachers, nurses, and other professionals.

Camps were set up for most of these poor homeless destitutes. One camp, much like other camps visited by Levi Coffin, shocked those of his group. They found it to be in deplorable condition, far worse than had been reported to him.

Chilly weather and lack of shelter brought sickness to many of these bedraggled scantily dressed individuals. No bedding nor cooking utensils, none of the comforts and few of the necessities of life could be seen. The only rations were what was supplied by the government.

The camp superintendent was a Baptist minister who fitted up the old barracks for better shelter and held religious meetings for the slaves. Another couple had left their home with the intention of opening a school among the coloreds. After five and one-half days, over fifty had learned the entire alphabet. It was reported that after learning the alphabet, many could spell words of three letters. Letters were sent out to friends and at once a collection of bedding, clothes, and money was begun.

The Western Freedmen's Aid Commission was formed in January of 1863, made up of different denominations in Cincinnati. Levi Coffin was appointed general agent of this commission and a warehouse was opened where supplies could be sent. General Grant gave free transportation for all supplies and for agents and teachers.

At Memphis, Tennessee there were three large colonies of freed people who were cultivating the ground with farming implements that had been sent to them. At one camp the people lived in tents and their church and school house was a shelter made of brush. These camps had a picket guard of colored men who kept a sharp lookout for rebel raiders.

Camps in the South were destroyed by the rebels, their cabins burned, and blacks had to leave, abandoning their gardens

Freedman camps

School for Freedmen

Chapter Twenty-Nine

Life for *Minty* after the Civil War

The Civil War is over. Minty is now a widow and nearly 80 years old. She and her son Milford and three grandchildren are living with her married daughter, Sarah Wilson in New Richmond. Lincoln has been assassinated. A grandson had been killed in the War. The slaves have been set free. Now it was time to pick up the pieces. Her thoughts often drifted southward to her old Kentucky home and the Green Clay family. It has been almost fifty years since she left behind eight of her children. She now has eighteen. And how many grandchildren and great grand children?

Hundreds of the freedmen had been resettled in camps right here in Ohio. Did some of these belong to her? Would she ever be reunited with them? What did life now hold for her? [Based on the census records, it appears that some of Minty's Kentucky family had moved to the Cincinnati area after being set free.]

Life for Minty has changed little, but many unsettling changes were in store for the blacks. They were free, but what did this new freedom look like for them? Although there were many skilled workers among them, jobs were scarce. No longer did the blacks have masters who provided for their food and shelter. They were on their own. Many free blacks found work as barbers, and some had small cook shops and grocery stores, which usually doubled as saloons and gambling houses. Most found menial, servile occupations as deckhands on steamboats or as porters on trains. Incomes were often insufficient to support the family, so the women were forced to work as well. The women found work as cooks, laundresses, housekeepers, and peddlers. Two of Minty's granddaughters worked in the insane asylum where another granddaughter was a patient.

Many things occurred which hindered them from enjoying their so-called freedom. The war was over, but there was still another war to be fought. That was a war of gaining equality with the whites. That was a period in history when there was much violence against the blacks.

Fear continually haunted these free blacks, fear of never knowing when their homes might be burnt or one of them might be hung. As the whites moved into the suburbs, the mulattos moved into the old white neighborhoods and the darker blacks settled in less attractive areas and were concentrated most heavily in "Bucktown", a poor undesirable neighborhood near the riverfront, with little sanitation and a generally unhealthy environment. This was largely caused from the slaughterhouses that dumped discarded intestines on the above hillsides.

Blacks after the Civil War enjoyed many privileges that their predecessors could only dream of. They could vote, hold office and attend school. However, new laws restricted what was to be freedom. First of all, the Black Codes which placed taxes on free blacks who tried to pursue nonagricultural professions, restricted the abilities of blacks to rent land or own guns, and even allowed the children of "unfit" parents to be apprenticed to the old slave masters. The fight for black rights would be a long one. The Black Codes allowed for the arrest of blacks who were unemployed and blacks were treated just as badly after the war as they were before the war. In effect, this was a continuation of slavery. Also, it was during this time period that anti-black groups, such as the Ku Klux Klan, reared their ugly heads.

Blacks were not given anywhere near the freedoms they expected to gain out of the Civil War. Although the Fourteenth Amendment, which was intended to provide the newly freed slaves with equal rights, was passed, it did not have much of an impact on African American rights, as blacks were the victims of the Black Codes and Jim Crow Laws. The Supreme Court upheld the practice of segregation, making it even more difficult for blacks to remove themselves from their low position on the social ladder.

The Jim Crow laws segregated everything in society, from drinking fountains to restaurants to seating in buses and trains. When the constitutionality of these practices was brought to the Supreme Court in the case of Plessy v. Ferguson, the Supreme Court upheld the practice of segregation, saying that it was not discriminatory if the facilities were "separate but equal." This ruling gave the green light on segregation, which made it seem as if treating blacks differently was an okay thing to do. People continued to feel that blacks were inferior and they weren't even good enough to use the same restrooms and sit in the same areas on buses.

Many slaves acquired new names to replace those given them by their masters, and they required whites to address them by "Mr." and "Mrs." They formed their own churches which became the center of their community. They also became educated with the help of white societies and the Freedmen's Bureau. To many, a top priority was to be reunited with the separated family members. They searched for their loved ones. But how could they accomplish this?

For Minty, life continued on without the interruptions faced by so many others. She had continued working as a domestic after Lewis died in 1860, and she still cleaned a Sunday School room at the Cranston Memorial Presbyterian Church in New Richmond.

In 1880 Minty was found again as head of the household with three grand children living with her. Anderson worked as a steamboat deckhand, Thomas, a porter, and Laura, a domestic. Other family members worked as waiters, laundresses, or elevator operators.

Minty died on Friday, January 6, 1898 at Sophia Street, New Richmond, Clermont Co., Ohio. She was known and respected not only for her old age, but also for her excellence of character and none but will regret her death. She had a great grandson in War of 1898, who was killed at Santiago. "Though wrinkled and grey, she retained excellent health up to the day of her death when the machinery of life, worn to a thread, stopped, and she passed to her reward."

At the time of Minty's death, her daughter Sarah (O'Banion) Wilson was living in New Richmond. Her son, Milton, age 62 was also living in New Richmond, as well as a grandson, G.W. O'Banion.

Minty is buried in the Samarian Cemetery, just down the road from the Cranston Memorial Presbyterian Church.

At the time of Minty's death , she was living on Sophia Street in New Richmond. See the maps below and on the next pages.

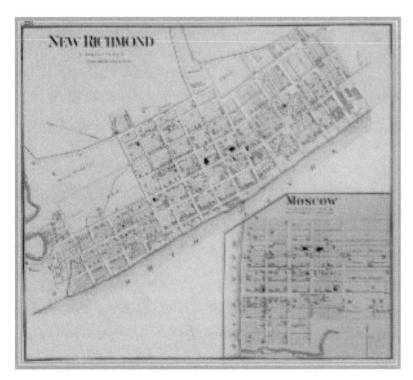

Map showing Minty's last home address

Map showing Minty's last home address

Unbelievable, yet true! Minty O'Banion, a slave for nearly thirty years and then a domestic for another eighty years, had been born and raised in an environment of the elite. Her owners, and then her employers, were famous and powerful men, some the fathers of our country. Daily she would come face to face with them. As she busily went about her domestic duties of caring for their needs, she listened and learned. She saw them at their best and she saw them at their worst. She

Aerial map showing Minty's last home address

quietly shared in their heartaches and disappointments, and she quietly shared in their achievements. She raised her own children and she nurtured many not her own, some who would become famous. Her life was a life filled with service to others, some forced upon her, some as a free employee, and some as her contribution. Although unable to either read or write, her head was filled with the history of our country, a history that was gained firsthand through experience.

No longer would she be seen shuffling fee- bly along the shoreline, stooping slowly to pick up the slivered driftwood, each piece resurrecting a tearful memory that brought about a change to the nation.

A possible likeness of an aged Minty O'Banion

A Tribute to Aunt Minty

Born as a slave and lived as a slave For years twenty-eight.

Then freedom set in and new life began At home in a brand new state.

Tears trickled down her cheeks. Thoughts of loved ones left behind

Would be closely tied in her bosom, And never leave her mind.

No longer bound to a Massa Would she be inclined; But now as an employee,

New freedom she would find.

Point Pleasant became her new home, With the Grants she would abide;

And soon a little boy

Would be placed at her side.

Many dignitaries had she met, Many new ones still to come, Many chil-

luns on the horizon Before her life was done.

Continual work as a domestic, Raising her own and grandchildren as

well; Gathering wood along the shoreline Until the toll of the bell.

A life lived long,

A charitable soul was she; Now home with her Maker She would ever be.

Minty's *Presidents* and Their Views on *Slavery*

*A*rminta O'Banion lived her 111 years under the administrations of twenty-four presidents. Each of these individuals had his own view as to slavery.

George Washington

Minty was born on January 6, 1788, just before George Washington became the first president of the United States under the Constitution (1789-1797).

During Washington's administration Minty was given to Susan Randolph as her personal slave. She was acquainted with Washington personally because of her mistress,

Susan Randolph, and Washington's granddaughter, Nellie Parke Custis. Washington owned 22 slaves when he took over Mount Vernon, and gained 200 more when he married Martha Dandridge Custis. By 1786 he owned 216. Martha's personal slave, Oney Judge, ran away and never returned. In Washington's will, he freed his manservant, William Lee, and gave him a pension. His other slaves were to be set free when Martha died. The dower slaves could not be legally set free because they belonged to the Custis estate.

Washington's feelings toward slavery can be seen in his quote: "I can only say that no man living wishes more sincerely than I do to see the abolition of (slavery). … But when slaves who are happy & content to remain with their present masters, are tampered with & seduced to leave them … it introduces more evils than it can cure."

John Adams

John Adams followed Washington as president (1797-1801). There is no record of Adams owning any slaves. He said: "I shudder when I think of the calamities which slavery is likely to produce in this country. You would think me mad if I were to describe my anticipations. If the gangrene is not stopped I can see nothing but insurrection of the blacks against the whites."

Thomas Jefferson

The third president, Thomas Jefferson (1801-1809), had inherited many slaves and his wife brought a dowry of more than 100 slaves. He later purchased more and at some points he was one of the largest slave owners in Virginia. In 1790 he gave his daughter and her husband 1,000 acres of land and 25 slaves, in 1798 he owned 141 slaves, mostly elderly, and in 1800 he owned 93. One of his slaves, Sally Hemings, allegedly the half-sister of his deceased wife, was reported to be his mistress. She was the mother of six children. Although a slave owner, Jefferson was a consistent opponent of slavery his whole life, calling it a "moral depravity" and a "hideous blot" which presented the greatest threat to the survival of the new nation. In 1778 he drafted a Virginia law that prohibited the importation of enslaved Africans, and in 1784, proposed an ordinance banning slavery in the Northwest Territories.

Minty may well have been in the appearance of Jefferson, what with his close association with the Washingtons and the Randolphs. Also, early into Jefferson's administration, Minty was loaned to Green Clay to become a part of his breeding of a "new crop".

James Madison

The next president, James Madison (1809-1817), grew up in a slave-owning family and owned slaves all his life. In 1833 he sold several of his farms but not his slaves. A year later he sold 16 slaves to a relative—with their permission. He did not free his slaves in his will. He states his feelings about slavery:

"A general emancipation of slaves ought to be 1. gradual. 2. equitable & satisfactory to the individuals immediately concerned. 3. consistent with the existing & durable prejudices of the nation...To be consistent with existing and probably unalterable prejudices in the U.S. freed blacks ought to be permanently removed beyond the region occupied by or allotted to a white population."

During Madison's presidency, Minty had been relocated to the Green Clay plantation, married to Lewis O'Banion, and became the mother of several children. She supposedly had become part of the slave breeding economy.

James Monroe

Our fifth president was James Monroe (1817-1825). Monroe inherited a slave named Ralph. When he owned the farm Highland he owned 30 to 40 slaves. His view of slavery in his words was "We perceive an existing evil which commenced under our Colonial system, with which we are not properly chargeable, or if at all not in the present degree, and we acknowledge the extreme difficulty of remedying it."

While Monroe was president, Minty again changed her location. She and Louis had been set free by General Green Clay and removed to Point Pleasant, Ohio where she became employed by Jesse Grant, father of the infamous General and later president, Ulysses S. Grant. She nurtured the infant Grant, witnessed his youthful escapades, and kept track of his journey through life.

John Quincy Adams

John Quincy Adams came next (1825-1829). He owned no slaves. He expressed his feelings this way: "What can I do for the cause of God and man, for the progress of human emancipation, for the suppression of the African slave-trade? Yet my conscience presses me on; let me but die upon the breach." During his administration, Minty continued living with the Grants in Georgetown.

Andrew Jackson

Andrew Jackson followed Adams to the White House (1829-1837). Jackson bought his first slave, a young woman, in 1788, the year Minty was born. By 1794 his business included slave trading and he had purchased at least 16 slaves. In the 1820's Jackson owned about 160 slaves. He did not free his slaves in his will. He made the statement: "As far as lenity can be extended to these unfortunate creatures I wish you to do so; subordination must be obtained first, and then good treatment." During Jackson's administration, a saddened Minty left the Grants after about fourteen years (1834), the children, and especially Ulysses, having come to seem like her own. Minty's life so far seems to have been that of leaving loved ones behind. She and Lewis moved to Bethel where she worked for the Morris, Birney, and Beecher families. While at the Birneys, she witnessed the harassment experienced by Birney, with his printing press being destroyed twice.

Martin Van Buren

Next came Martin Van Buren (1837-1841). He owned slaves, but not while he was president. When he was young his father owned six. Martin's only slave, Tom, ran away in about 1814. When Tom was found eight years later, Martin offered him for sale to the finder for $50. Van Buren said, "Before the election I declared that: I must go into the Presidential chair the inflexible and uncompromising opponent of every attempt on the part of Congress to abolish slavery in the District of Columbia against the wishes of the slaveholding

States, and also with a determination equally decided to resist the slightest interference with it in the States where it exists."

Minty, at this time, still worked in various homes in the Cincinnati area, some of which included the Beecher and Birney families. During this administration, Lewis was baptized in 1839 and Minty in 1840 and both were sextons at the Cranston Memorial Presbyterian Church in Point Pleasant, Ohio.

Also, at the beginning of this administration, New York City hosted the first Convention of the Anti-Slavery Society of American Women, an event attended by both black and white women. In Philadelphia in 1838, proslavery mobs rioted against this society. In 1840, Texas prohibited slaves from carrying weapons without written permission, and South Carolina enacted a Black Code by which slaves were denied the rights to assemble, produce food, earn money, learn to read, and to possess any clothing but low- quality garments.

William Henry Harrison

The following president, William Henry Harrison (1841), served for only thirty days. He owned slaves, but not while president. His father and grandfather owned many slaves. Harrison took seven of them with him to the Northwest Territory in 1800 where slavery was illegal. They then became indentured servants on terms undistinguishable from slavery.

In 1801 he purchased a runaway slave and later freed him. He stayed on as a servant for many years.

He was appointed Governor of Indiana Territory, which was "free soil". He attempted to have slavery made legal there, but generally followed the law by keeping Blacks as indentured servants who were free after about a decade of service. His feelings were expressed this way: "We cannot emancipate the slaves of the other states without their consent … except by producing a convulsion which would undo us all. We must wait the slow but certain progress of those good principles which are everywhere gaining ground, and which, assuredly will ultimately prevail."

Pneumonia, developed from a cold, took this president's life before he could do anything about the slavery issue. This brought to Minty memories of another president dying.

John Tyler

Harrison's vice president, John Tyler took office (1841-1845). He owned slaves. His feelings were expressed as: "(God) works most inscrutably to the understandings of men; the Negro is torn from Africa, a barbarian, ignorant and idolatrous; he is restored, civilized, enlightened, and a Christian."

During this time, Minty was working for the Beechers, becoming close to Harriett Beecher Stowe. She and Lewis had supplied her with information for her novel, *Uncle Tom's Cabin*, which she had begun to write.

James Polk

James Polk became the next president (1845-1849). In 1832 he had fifteen slaves. His view of slavery is shown in his words: "The slave dreads the punishment of stripes (i.e. whippings) more than he does imprisonment, and that description of punishment has, besides, a beneficial effect upon his fellow slaves."

Levi Coffin, president of the Underground Railroad, entered Minty's life about this time, and Minty found herself and her family right in the midst of much heartache and turmoil for escaping slaves.

Virginia passed a law permitting emancipation of any slave by will or deed, and Kentucky removed restraints on intrastate slave trade, whereas South Carolina removed restraints on interstate slave trade.

Zachary Taylor

The twelfth president, Zachary Taylor (1849-1850), owned slaves. His father owned 26 slaves in 1800. In 1847, Zachary owned more than 100 slaves. He supposedly never sold any slaves. He said, "So far as slavery is concerned, we of the south must throw ourselves on the Constitution and defend our rights under it to the last, and when arguments will no longer suffice, we will appeal to the sword, if necessary."

Minty continued working in the Cincinnati area for these several abolitionist families. She was once again saddened by Harriet Beecher Stowe moving to Maine. Harriet's book was about to be published.

Millard Fillmore

Millard Fillmore (1849-1853) became the thirteenth president. He owned no slaves. He expressed his feelings this way: "God knows that I detest slavery, but it is an existing evil, for which we are not responsible, and we must endure it, and give it such protection as is guaranteed by the Constitution, till we can get rid of it without destroying the last hope of free government in the world."

Virginia demanded that emancipated slaves leave the state within a year and forbid the legislature from freeing any slave.

Sojourner Truth gave her famous "Ain't I a Woman" speech. Radical abolitionist John Brown and his followers struck in retaliation to pro-slavery groups in Kansas by attacking the town of Lawrence.

Franklin Pierce

The fourteenth president, Franklin Pierce (1853-1857), owned no slaves. His viewpoint was this: "The citizens of New Hampshire are no more responsible, morally or politically, for the existence of this domestic institution (slavery) in Virginia or Maryland, than he would be for the existence of any similar institutions in France or Persia. Why? Because these are matters over which the States … retained the exclusive and sole control, and for which they are alone responsible … It is admitted that domestic slavery exists here (Washington, D.C.) in its mildest form. That part of the population is bound together by friendship and the nearer relations of life. They are attached to the families in which they have lived from childhood. They are comfortably provided for, and apparently contented."

During Franklin Pierce's administration, the Supreme Court denied citizenship to all slaves, ex-slaves, and descendants of slaves and the right to prohibit slavery in the territories acquired after the creation of the United States.

James Buchanan

The next president was James Buchanan, (1857-1861). The slave population had grown to nearly four million, making the ratio of free to enslaved Americans approximately 7:1.

He condemned slavery as immoral, and argued that freeing them would result in greater evil. Buchanan, the fifteenth president, technically owned no slaves; however, he discovered that his sister's husband owned two slaves in Virginia. He purchased them immediately, converting them to indentured servants. Daphne Cook, aged 22, was indentured for seven years. Ann Cook, age 5, was indentured for 23 years. He made the statement: "The natural tendency of their publications is to produce dissatisfaction and revolt among the slaves, and to incite their wild passions to vengeance … Many a mother clasps her infant to her bosom when she retires to rest, under dreadful apprehensions that she may be aroused from her slumbers by the savage yells of the slaves by whom she is surrounded. These are the words of the abolitionists."

Abraham Lincoln

Abraham Lincoln (1861-1865), the 16th president, is considered one of the greatest presidents. He owned no slaves. He said, " I have always thought that all men should be free; but if any be slaves it should be first those who desire it for themselves, and secondly those who desire it for others. Whenever I hear anyone arguing for slavery I feel a strong impulse to see it tried on him personally."

During his administration, South Carolina secedes from the Union, followed by Mississippi, Florida, Alabama, Georgia, Louisiana, and Texas. Later in the year, Virginia, Arkansas,

Tennessee, and North Carolina. The Union of Confederate states was formed and Jefferson Davis was elected its president

The Civil War began and 75,000 blacks volunteered for the U.S. army, but were rejected, including Minty's grandsons. Congress abolished slavery in Washington D.C. and the territories.

Lincoln signed the Homestead Act which gave public land to qualified private citizens, including black heads of house over 21 years old and single black women. The Militia Act authorized the President to employ all persons, including blacks, in the military or naval service and gave enemy-owned slaves freedom in return for service to Union forces. The South followed suit.

Lincoln issued the Emancipation Proclamation, freeing all slaves in areas of rebellion. The 54th Massachusetts Colored Infantry was organized. It was the first black regiment in the Free states. Black soldiers were recruited and trained across the North.

The Fugitive Slave Law was repealed and Black soldiers protested unequal compensation and were promised equal pay. Several southern states abolished slavery. .

During his presidency the Freedmen's Bureau was set up in 1864 in the war-ravaged South for the purpose of providing emergency food, housing, and medical aid to black and white refugees. It also helped to reunite families divided by slave sales and to adjust to new conditions. The Thirteenth Amendment to the U.S. Constitution abolished slavery throughout the country.

General Lee surrendered to General Grant at the Appomattox Court House in Virginia. Lincoln was assassinated.

Andrew Johnson

Andrew Johnson followed Lincoln (1865-1869). He owned slaves, but not while he was president. He bought his first slave, a manservant named Sam, in 1837. He eventually owned eight. He owned slaves at the beginning of the Civil War. He said that some of them came back voluntarily after being confiscated by the Confederates, and these he treated as freemen. If he didn't free all of his individually he certainly freed them in 1864 when, as military governor in Tennessee, he proclaimed freedom for all slaves in the state. He said, "You tell me, friends, of the liberation of the colored people of the South. But have you thought of the millions of Southern white people who have been liberated by the war?

Several laws were passed to assist the transition of slaves to new freedom, race riots took place, and the Ku Klux Klan was founded. More states were readmitted to the Union. The Fourteenth Amend- ment to the Constitution gave blacks equal protection under the law, and the Fifteenth Amendment to the U.S. Constitution secured the right to vote for black male adults.

Ulysses S. Grant

The war was expensive to the South, as well as to the North, both in blood and treasure, but it was worth all it cost. General Grant was an extraordinarily responsible and devoted father and husband. He was extremely loving and kind towards his wife and children and was always considered a hero in the eyes of his family. Perhaps General Grant was the most ethical and moral family man and U. S. President that we ever had.

Minty beamed with pride when her Ulysses became her president. She hungrily listened for any news of him and his family.

During Grant's administration was seen the first black American diplomat, the first black elected to the House of Representatives and the first black elected to the U.S. Senate. Also, for the first time, African Americans were listed by name in a U.S. Census.

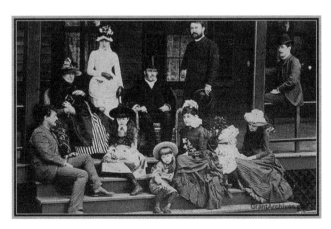

The Grant family

General Grant, his son, and his wife

Rutherford B. Hayes

Rutherford B. Hayes (1877-1881) the last of the Reconstruction Era brought blacks to a second class citizenship with limited rights.

James A. Garfield

James A. Garfield (1881) He supported education for black southerners and called for African American suffrage.

Chester A. Arthur

Chester A. Arthur (1881-1885) on occasion, sent in the military to protect African Americans from newly formed terrorist groups, such as the Ku Klux Klan, which tried to prevent blacks from participating in society. He helped defend the FIRST black woman to refuse to give up her seat on a bus (horse drawn) in 1854.

Grover Cleveland

Grover Cleveland (1885-1889). Cleveland, like a growing number of Northerners (and nearly all white Southerners) saw Reconstruction as a failed experiment, and was reluctant to use federal power to enforce the 15th Amendment of the U.S. Constitution, which guaranteed voting rights to African Americans. Though Cleveland appointed no black Americans to patronage jobs, he allowed Frederick Douglass to continue in his post as recorder of deeds in Washington, D.C. and appointed another black man to replace Douglass upon his resignation.

Benjamin Harrison

Benjamin Harrison (1889-1893). After regaining the majority in both Houses of Congress, some Republicans, led by Harrison, attempted to pass legislation to protect black Americans' civil rights. Harrison's Attorney General, William H. H. Miller, through the Justice Department, ordered the prosecutions for violation of voting rights in the South; however, white juries often failed to convict or indict violators. This prompted Harrison to urge Congress to pass legislation that would "secure all our people a free exercise of the right of suffrage and every other civil right under the Constitution and laws". "The colored people did not intrude themselves upon us; they were brought here in chains and held in communities where they are now chiefly bound by a cruel slave code... when and under what conditions is the black man to have a free ballot? When is he in fact to have those full civil rights which have so long been his in law? When is that quality of influence which our form of government was intended to secure to the electors to be restored?"

He severely questioned the states' civil rights records, arguing that if states have the authority over civil rights, then "we have a right to ask whether they are at work upon it." Harrison also supported a bill proposed by Senator Henry W. Blair, which would have granted federal funding to schools regardless of the students' races. He also endorsed a proposed constitutional amendment to overturn the 1883 Supreme Court rulings that declared much of the Reconstruction-era Civil Rights Acts unconstitutional. None of these measures gained congressional approval.

William McKinley

William McKinley (1897-1901) Minty's last president. In the wake of McKinley's election in 1896, African Americans were hopeful of progress towards equality. McKinley had spoken out against lynching while governor, and most African Americans who could vote supported him in 1896. McKinley's priority, however, was in ending sectionalism, and they were disappointed by his policies and appointments. Although McKinley made some appointments of African Americans to low-level government posts, and received some praise for that, the appointments were less than they had received under previous Republican administrations. The response of the administration's response to racial violence was minimal. According to historian Clarance A. Bacote, "Before the Spanish– American War, the Negroes, in spite of some mistakes, regarded McKinley as the best friend they ever had." African Americans saw the onset of war in 1898 as an opportunity to display their patriotism; and black soldiers fought bravely at El Caney and San Juan Hill.

It was during this war that a second grandson of Minty was killed in action.

First Ladies

It is known how the presidents viewed slavery, but what about the first ladies? It appears that only one could be considered an advocate of abolition along with her husband. This was Louisa Adams, wife of John Adams. She aided her husband in circulating letters and publications advocating the abolition of slavery. A second first lady, Mary Lincoln, became a supporter and contributor of the Freedman's Bureau, an organization which helped find housing, education, and employment for freed African- American slaves.

As far as concern for the Blacks, Lucy Hayes supported several institutions that aided orphans, the education of Native American and African American girls, and Civil War veterans. Another, Frances Cleveland, was a board member and active organizer of the Washington Club a charitable club that aided indigent African-American children of Washington, D.C.

Did You Know This About Minty's *Presidents?*

George Washington

Thinking that shaking hands was beneath the dignity of the President, Washington preferred to bow to greet guests. To avoid being forced into a handshake he would place one hand on his sword and hold his hat in the other.

Millard Fillmore

Millard Fillmore installed the first bathtub and kitchen stove in the White House.

When Millard Fillmore moved into the White House, it didn't have a Bible. He and his wife, Abigail, installed the first library.

John Adams

John Adams was the first to live in the White House.

Thomas Jefferson

Thomas Jefferson spoke six different languages.

James Madison

James Madison was the smallest president, 5' and 4" and under 100 pounds.

Abraham Lincoln

Lincoln was the first president to be assassinated.

Rutherford B. Hayes

Rutherford B. Hayes was the first president to use a telephone. His number was Number 1.

James Garfield

James Garfield could write with both hands at the same time, each with a different language.

Zachary Taylor

Zachary Taylor died from contracting cholera from a bowl of cherries washed down with iced milk.

Franklin Pierce

Franklin Pierce, while President, was arrested for running over an old woman with his horse.

Abraham Lincoln

Abraham Lincoln was a notably ugly man in photos but people who met him described his face as intelligent and handsome in motion. The first President to wear a beard he grew it at the suggestion of a young girl, Grace Bedell, who wrote to him.

Andrew Johnson

Andrew Johnson was drunk at Lincoln's second inauguration. The event was described by a senator as follows. "The inauguration went off very well except that the Vice President Elect was too drunk to perform his duties & disgraced himself & the Senate by making a drunken foolish speech. I was never so mortified in my life, had I been able to find a hole I would have dropped through it out of sight."

Ulysses S. Grant

Ulysses S. Grant gained a reputation for drinking heavily while still a young man. When President Lincoln was warned about Grant's drinking habits during the civil war he is supposed to have responded "If it makes fighting men like Grant, then find out what he drinks, and send my other commanders a case!"

Chester A. Arthur

Chester A. Arthur changed his pants several times a day. He owned 80 pair of pants.

Grover Cleveland

Grover Cleveland was the first president to be married in the White House.

Grant's Wife's Family

Grant's wife's family were slave owners and Grant himself owned a slave named William Jones, given to him by his father-in-law. At a time when Grant could have badly used the money from selling Jones, he signed a document that freed him instead.

Ulysses S. Grant

As president, Grant was arrested by a police officer who failed to recognize him. He was fined $20 for speeding in his horse and buggy and had to go back to the White House on foot.

George Washington

Washington's teeth were made from elephant and walrus tusks, not wood.

James Garfield

James Garfield could write Latin with his left hand whilst simultaneously writing Greek with his right

Benjamin Harrison

Benjamin Harrison, while in office, had electricity installed in the White House. Unfortunately he and his wife were terrified of it and would not touch switches for fear of electrocution and often slept with the lights on.

John Adams

As a young boy, John Adams would often skip school, choosing instead to spend his time hunting and fishing.

Andrew Jackson

Andrew Jackson was the first president to ride on a train.

Martin Van Buren

Martin Van Buren was the first president born an American citizen. The others were all born in the British colonies.

William Henry Harrison

William Henry Harrison was president for only 31 days. He died of pneumonia.

John Tyler

John Tyler loved children. He and his wife had 15 children.

Andrew Jackson

Andrew Jackson taught his parrot to swear. The parrot had to be removed from President Jackson's funeral because it wouldn't stop swearing.

John Quincy Adams

John Quincy Adams was fond of swimming naked in the Potomac. When an intrepid female reporter wished to get an interview with the President she stole his clothes until he agreed to an interview.

It Is True

Civil War Dead

Most Civil War dead were not returned home for interment. Many bodies were ground into the earth by horse hooves or wagon wheels and thousands drowned. Square hits from artillery shredded bodies. After several battles, soldiers recalled seeing bodies eaten by hogs. The U.S. Army did not start issuing dog tags until 1906.

Most Common Operation

The most common operation performed on soldiers during the Civil War was amputation. The best surgeon could have a limb severed and discarded within five minutes. Civil War doctors were nicknamed "sawbones." There were 60,000 partial or complete amputations during the war.

African American Nurse

Susie King Taylor, a runaway slave from Georgia and Civil War nurse, was one of the first African American nurses in United States history. She also taught soldiers to read and write.

Dr. Mary Edwards

Dr. Mary Edwards was the first woman awarded the Medal of Honor.

Syphilis and Gonorrhea

Among Union white troops, surgeons treated over 73,000 soldiers for syphilis and over 109,000 for gonorrhea. African American soldiers had incidences of less than half that of the white troops.

Goverment-Sanctioned Prositution

Because of the epidemic of venereal diseases among soldiers, the Union army tried government-sanctioned prostitution in Nashville and Memphis from 1863 to1865. The incidence of venereal disease declined sharply.

"I Flow Away"

During the Civil War, diarrhea (Greek, meaning "I flow away") was the most common and deadly disease. More Civil War soldiers died from diarrhea than were killed in battle. About 1 in 40 cases was fatal. Death came from dehydration, exhaustion, or the rupture of the intestinal wall.

Mercury Used As Medicine

The cure-all medicine for the Civil War was calomel, a mercury mixture of chalk, honey and sometimes licorice. It was used to treat everything from syphilis to headaches. When one Union army doctor, William Hammond, noted that mercury was poisonous, he was dismissed as a quack and removed from his post.

APPENDIX

Civil War fatalities

On average, of every 100 fatalities on the battlefield, five men died from limb wounds, 12 from punctures to the lower abdomen, 15 from damage to the heart or liver, and more than 50 from lacerations to the head or neck.

Slave Marriages

Did you know that slave marriages were not considered legal or binding by judges, lawyers, or masters, black or white? They were recognized in no southern state. Families could be legally separated as desired by owners. One-third of all slave unions were broken by sale; however, most slave owners did recognize the importance of such unions. Owners recognized the value of the increase in population, as well as the threat of separation kept slave population under control.

Civil War Horses

In a single day, the one million Civil War horses would have peed enough urine to fill more than 12 standard swimming pools.

Draft Animals Life Expectancy

Horses and other draft animals had about a 7-month life expectancy during the Civil War. As many as 300,000 horses died. More than 3,000 horses were killed at Gettysburg alone.

General Nathan Bedford

General Nathan Bedford Forrest, CSA, had twenty-nine horses shot from beneath him during the war years.

Horse and Mule Fatalities

Over 3,000,000 horses and mules were killed during the Civil War. Nick Nicholls, Civil War historian, basing his more than 30 years of collecting information, said, "It is my considered opinion that a reasonable estimate of the equine mortality rate, not including wounded equines during the Civil War to be between 1,350,000 and 1,500,000."

Bloodiest War

The Civil War was the bloodiest war ever fought on American soil. During an average day during the war, approximately 600 people were killed. By the end of the war, over 618,000 people had died. This is more Americans than WWI, WWII, the Korean War, and the Vietnam War combined.

The Youngest Soldier

The youngest soldier in the Civil War was a 9-year-old boy from Mississippi. The oldest was an 80-year-old from Iowa. More than 10,000 soldiers serving in the Union Army were under 18 years old. [from Images of the Civil War]

Daniel Emmett

Daniel Emmett, the composer of "Dixie" was not only from the North, but he was also a loyal Unionist. He was disgusted by the song's popularity in the South. Lincoln claimed that it was one of "the best tunes I ever heard."

Decoration Day

The last Southern troops surrendered on May 26, 1865. Afterward, survivors began decorating the graves of those who had died. They repeated the ritual each year on "The Decoration Day"—which is now known as Memorial Day.

APPENDIX

Divorce Rate

In the 20 years after the Civil War, the national divorce rate increased 150%.

Prison Camp Elmira

The Civil War prison camp Elmira had two observation towers constructed for onlookers. Citizens paid 15 cents to look at the inmates. Concession stands by the towers sold peanuts, cakes, and lemonade while the men inside starved.

Military Age Men

In the North, more than 1/3 of all men of military age served in the war. For the South, it was nearly 2/3.

Marching Miles

Most Civil War soldiers marched 15 to 20 miles a day.

A "Butcher"

Ulysses S. Grant's critics called him a "butcher" because of his high casualty rates in battle.

Names Of One War

The Civil War was known by more than 25 names, including "The Brothers War," "The War to Suppress Yankee Arrogance," "The War for the Union," and "The War of the Rebellion."

Female Soldiers

Although both the North and South did not allow women in the army, it is estimated that 250-400 women fought disguised as men.

Quaker Guns

"Quaker guns" (named for the pacifist religious group) were fake artillery that was used by both sides through the Civil War to cause confusion about troop location and strength.

Richard Gatling

Richard Gatling hoped his invention would end the war.

Brush Fires

An estimated 800 wounded men burned to death at the Battle of the Wilderness because they were unable to crawl away from advancing brush fires.

Wide Doorways

Centuries before and decades after the Civil War, including the war itself, doorways were wide, not because of the width of women's skirts, but so coffins could be passed through, with a pallbearer on either side.

Desertions

There were around 200,000 Civil War desertions from the estimated 85,000 Union men fled to Canada. Of the 76,000 deserters who were caught, almost all were returned to duty. Officially Union side and more than 120,000 from the Confederate ranks. 141 were executed.

African American Soldiers

Of the nearly 200,000 blacks who fought for the North, more than 100,000 were runaway slaves. The number of blacks who enlisted in the Union Army was larger than the number of soldiers in the entire Confederate Army in the final months of the war. Twenty-five African American soldiers were awarded the Congressional Medal of Honor. Approximately 35,000 of the nearly 200,000 died during the war.

Runaway Slaves

Before the Civil War, approximately 5,000 slaves attempted to escape per year. During the war, the number increased to 5,000 or more per month.

Robert E. Lee's Estate

During the war, the Union confiscated Robert E. Lee's estate and turned it into a cemetery so that he would be reminded of the carnage he caused. It later became Arlington National Cemetery.

Ulysses Grant

Ulysses Grant was the first president to have both his parents living as he entered office.

Camp Douglas

To prevent escape at Camp Douglas in Chicago, prisoners were not allowed to wear clothes. Even blankets were taken away. Many Confederates froze to death.

The Gettysburg Address

The Gettysburg Address revolutionized how Americans understood the Republic. Edward Everett, the main speaker at the Gettysburg dedication, spoke for two hours. President Abraham Lincoln, who was invited almost as an afterthought, spoke for two minutes. His speech went down in history.

APPENDIX

The Grants and Ford Theater

The Grants were to have accompanied the Lincolns to the theater but their plans were changed. Grant had been invited to go to Ford Theater with President Lincoln but he and his wife Julia decided to travel to New Jersey to visit their children instead. Had he attended, he may have been a target as well.

Assassination Plans

Booth had planned to have others assassinated as well as President Lincoln. These included Secretary of State William Seward, Vice President Andrew Johnson, and General Grant.

The Sight of Blood

Grant couldn't stand the sight of blood. Although he witnessed some of the bloodiest battles in history, Grant could not stand the sight of blood. Rare steak nauseated him and he was known to cook his meat to the point of charring.

10 Cigars A Day

Grant used around seven to ten cigars a day, although many of them he did not smoke, chewing on them instead. After a reporter wrote that Grant liked cigars, people began to send them to him as gifts. He received over 20,000, which may have contributed to his throat cancer.

Poor Investments

After his presidency he lost all his savings to a shady investment partner, leaving his family with nearly nothing. At the time, presidents were not given pensions and Grant had already forfeited his military pension when he became president. Mark Twain offered Grant a generous deal to write his memoirs and while terminally ill with cancer, Grant finished just days before his death. The memoirs sold over 300,000 copies and earned his family over $450,000. In 1958, Congress passed legislation establishing a pension for presidents.

Surrender Generosity

When Grant accepted the surrender of Confederate forces by his rival Robert E. Lee in April 1865, he generously allowed Confederate soldiers to retain their weapons and horses and return to their homes.

A Speeding Ticket

The 18th President of the United States was given a $20 speeding ticket for riding his horse too fast down a Washington street.

Failed Assassination Attemps

Lincoln was shot at—and almost killed—nearly two years before he was assassinated. Late one August evening, in 1863, after an exhausting day at the White House, Lincoln rode alone by horse to the Soldiers' Home, his family's summer residence. A private at the gate heard a shot ring out and, moments later, the horse galloped into the compound, with a bareheaded Lincoln clinging to his steed. Lincoln explained that a gunshot had gone off at the foot of the hill, sending the horse galloping so fast it knocked his hat off. Two soldiers retrieved Lincoln's hat, which had a bullet hole right through it. The president asked the guards to keep the incident under wraps; He didn't want to worry his wife Mary.

Newspaper Articles and Information from the Cranston Memorial Presbyterian *Church*

Cranston Memorial Presbyterian Church 1821 - 1993

Arminta O'banion, born January 6, 1788; oldest inhabitant of Ohio.

Two Clermont County newspapers and at least one Cincinnati paper carried the story when New Richmond resident, Mrs. Arminta O'Banion died on the last day of 1898, at what is variously reported as age 111 or so, *The Clermont Courier* of January 11, 1899, carried an article, here much abbreviated:

APPENDIX

"OLDEST INHABITANT OF OHIO DIES AT NEW RICHMOND, aged 111 years"

There are few persons in New Richmond who did not know and respect Aunt Minty O'Banion, not only from her great age, but from the excellence of her character; and all regret her death last Friday, January 6, on which day she reached the marvelous age of 111 years and 6 days, as shown by authentic records. She has lived through every administration from Washington to McKinley, and noted every war from 1812 to 1898. She was known as Aunt Minty O'Banion. Born on January 6, 1788 just 9 miles from Washington's home at Mt. Vernon, she was 11 years old when he died and witnessed the pomp and ceremony of his funeral. The next year, she went with her young mistress to Kentucky, where she was married to one of the slaves [Lewis O'Banion] on the plantation of General Clay. After the war [of 1812] was over, General Clay emancipated O'Banion, and purchasing Aunt Minty of her owner, made her free, and the two located at Point Pleasant, the home of Jesse Grant, and the birthplace of his illustrious son, Ulysses. She was a domestic in that home when President Grant was born and attended his infant life. Aunt Minty's husband worked at odd jobs. In 1834 they moved to New Richmond, where she was a servant in the home of James G. Birney, publisher of the abolitionist paper, The Philanthropist. She also worked for Rev. Lyman Beecher of Lane Seminary, where she was a favorite of his daughter, Harriet Beecher Stowe, author of Uncle Tom's Cabin. In the 1840's the O'Banions returned to New Richmond. Lewis O'Banion died during the Civil War. They had grandsons in the war on the Union side [one was killed at Petersburg, Virginia] and a great grandson was killed in the War of 1898 at Santiago. Though wrinkled and gray beyond imagination she retained excellent health up to the day of her death,

[End of newspaper article.]

The *Clermont Sun* carried a shorter story, which contained additional information that *"One of New Richmond's most eccentric characters, Aunt Minty O'Banion, colored, died at her home on Sophia Street, December 30, 1898, … age 111 years … mother of 18 children, the youngest of whom, Mrs. Wilson is about 60 years of age. Up to the last few months she was quite active and was frequently seen along the river front picking up drift wood and baskets of chips."* An unidentified Cincinnati newspaper stated that her daughter, Mrs. Wilson, was aged 75 years; that she *"has a grandson, Milton, also living at New Richmond and a great-grandson, G.W. O'Banion, living in Cincinnati."*

These news stories may have been a bit overdone, as was customary and accepted around the turn of the century, but we include them as being very interesting. A peek at census records for 1850-1900 reveals huge discrepancies in the ages of Mrs. O'Banion and her children. Often census takers did not bother to get the facts, and again, sometimes the individual gave false information to appear young for employment opportunities. T.P. White's funeral home handled the arrangements of her burial, and their records indicate that she died December 31, 1898, at the age of 106, and that she is buried in Good Samaritan Cemetery, a half mile out of New Richmond on St. Route 132. Our Presbyterian Church records show that her husband, Lewis O'Banion, was baptized into the church in 1839, and she in 1841. They were the church sextons from 1841 to 1846. There are entries in an old treasurer's book of small payments to them. There are also entries of Lewis O'Banion's contribution toward Rev. O.H. Newton's salary. In 1865 there is an entry that Mrs. O'Banion was paid 50 cents for cleaning the Sunday School room.

Whatever her age or interesting life experiences, we are grateful for the news articles and we wish we could have talked to her.

APPENDIX

Batavia, Ohio

The Oldest Inhabitant Of Ohio Dies at New Richmond, Aged 111 Years.

There are few persons in New Richmond who did not know and respect Aunt Minty O'Banion, not only for her great age, but from the excellence of her character, and none but will regret her death, which took place on Friday, January 6, on which day she reached the marvelous age of 111 years and 6 days, as shown by authentic records. Her past is linked with the history of some of the greatest politicians and warriors of the age, and she has lived through every administration from Washington to McKinley, and noted the progress of every war from 1812 to 1898. She was known as Aunt Minty O'Banion, and she was born on the plantation of Peyton Randolph in Virginia, January 6, 1788. The place of her birth was nine miles from Mt. Vernon, the home of Washington, and she was 11 years old when he died, and witnessed the pomp and ceremony of his funeral. The next year, one of her master's daughters, having married, she went with her young mistress to Kentucky, where she was married to one of the slaves on the plantation of General Green Clay, her husband being the valet of that officer, and accompanied him on his numerous campaigns in the war of 1812, to Fort Meigs in this State, and on other expeditions, Aunt Minty always being one of theparty. After the war was over General Clay emancipated O'Banion, and purchasing Aunt Minty of her owner, made her free, and the two located at Point Pleasant, the home of Jesse Grant, and the birthplace of his illustrious son, Ulysses, and was a domestic in the Grant family when General

Grant was born, and for a long time attended his infant life, guiding his footsteps, and soothing to sleep, on her broad bosom, the head of one designed to become world-famous as a warrior and ruler. She later moved with her husband to Bethel, where she was employed in the family of Senator Morris, who was U.S. Senator when Gen. Thomas L. Hamer was reading law, and a member of the Morris household. Later General Hamer, as a congressman, appointed Grant to West Point, as is well remembered. Aunt Minty's husband worked about at odd jobs, while she was employed as servant in various Clermont homes. In 1834 she moved to New Richmond, where, in the same year, James S. Birney began the publication of his abolition paper, known as The Philanthropist, Aunt Minty being a servant in his home. A year later Mr. Birney moved his paper to Cincinnati, with Aunt Minty continuing with the family. In Cincinnati the paper was mobbed and the type scattered to the four winds. Subsequently Aunt Minty became a member of the household of Rev. Lyman Beecher of Lane Seminary, where she became a favorite of Harriet Beecher Stowe, supplying that brilliant writer with valuable data for her novel of Uncle Tom's Cabin, and giving her ideas of the darkey idioms and superstitions. Sometime in the forties the O'Banions returned to New Richmond, the husband dying during the Civil War, in which this celebrated character had three grandsons on the Union side, one of them having been killed at Petersburg, Virginia. She had a great grandson in the war of 1898 who was killed at Santiago.

—from the same paper under the New Richmond news:

One of New Richmond's most eccentric characters, Aunt Minty O'Banion, colored, died at her home on Sophia Street, Friday night, December 30, 1898. As near as can be ascertained she was born about 1788, and lived to the good old age of 110. She was the mother of eighteen children, the youngest of whom, Mrs. Wilson, is about sixty years of age. Up to within the last few months she was quite active and was frequently seen along the river front picking up driftwood and basket of chips, although she lost her mental powers years ago. The oldest citizens of the town unite in saying that she was a very old lady when they were in their youth. About fifty years ago she was janitress of one of our principal churches, and has always been numbered among the best of our colored citizens.

Bibliography

Ancestry.com

The Autobiography of Martin Luther King, Jr. Warner
Book, Inc.

Benton, William, publisher, Encyclopedia Britannica,
The University of Chicago, 1966.

Brady, Patricia, George Washington's Beautiful Nellie, the
University of South Carolina Press, 1991.

Buckmaster, Henriett, Flight to Freedom, Vail-Ballow
Press, Inc., Binghamton, New York, 1958.

Clarke, Duncan, The History of American Slavery, J.G.
Press PRC Publishing LTD., London S.W. 6 4N2, printed
in China ISBN

Coffin, Levi, Reminiscences of Levi Coffin, the Reputed
President of the Underground Railroad, Bibliobazaar.

Davies, William C., Brother Against Brother, Time Life
Books, Alexandria, Virginia, 1946.

Frederick Douglas, 1879.

Hollins, Sonya Bernard, New Light Shed on Monument.

BIBLIOGRAPHY

Battle Creek Enquirer, Aug. 21, 2002.

"I Have a Dream", Time Life Books, New York Library of Congress-6829113, pp. 38-40 (pictures).

Lewes, David L., King, A Critical Biography, Raeger Publishers, New York-Washington.

Macy, Jesse, The Anti-Slavery Crusade, The Abraham Lincoln Edition, Volume 28, New Haven: Yale University, 1919.

National Geographic. National Geographic Society, Washington, D.C., Vol. 166, July, 1984.

Pettit, E.M., Underground Railroad Sketches, Fredonia, N.Y.

Richardson, Albert D., The Field, the Dungeon, and the Escape. American Publishing Co., Hartford, Conn., 1865.

Stowe, Harriet Beecher, Uncle Tom's Cabin, London: Nathaniel Cooke, Milford House Strand, 1853.

Whitt, Aileen M., C.G.R.S., Cranston Memorial Presbyterian Church 1821-1993, New Richmond, Ohio.

Wier, Albert E., ed., The Songs of Stephen Foster, Harcourt, Brace, and Co., New York, 1935

Census Records

Newspaper obituaries

Numerous articles and pictures considered Public Domain on the Internet on the Randolphs, the Washingtons, the Green Clays, Jesse Grants, Morris, Birney, the Beechers, Levi Coffin, Rankin, Parker, the Civil War, Slavery in America, etc.